NICHOLAS COUNTY, KENTUCKY

1810-1840 CENSUSES

Transcribed By

Rowena Lawson

HERITAGE BOOKS, INC.

1984

Published By

HERITAGE BOOKS, INC.
3602 Maureen Lane
Bowie, MD 20715

ISBN 0-917890-39-6

INTRODUCTION

Nicholas County, Kentucky was formed in 1799 from parts of Bourbon and Mason counties. The county seat is at Carlisle. Unfortunately no census records exist for the parent counties for the 1790 and 1800 counts. Apparently they were destroyed during the British attack on Washington in the War of 1812.

The transcriptions which follow were made from microfilm copies of the extant censuses. Each census lists the name of the head of the household followed by statistical data showing the age categories of the various household members, including slaves and free colored. The statistical data was made more detailed in successive censuses making more columns necessary.

These early censuses provide only a partial listing of the adult, white-male population. Adult, white-females and blacks of either sex are not listed, except in the small proportion of cases where they are the head of a household. Although slaves are shown by age groupings in the latter censuses, they are not shown by name and have been listed here simply as a total number in the second column from the right. Free colored are likewise shown as a total number in the right-most column in each census.

The statistical data for the 1810 census consists of five columns on the left for men and five columns on the right for women followed by a column for slaves and a column for free colored. The age brackets for both men and women are (reading from left to right): under 10, 10 to 16, 16 to 26, 26 to 45, and 45 and over. The 1820 data is in the same arrangement, except that a column has been inserted for males aged 16 to 18. Note that means that males 16, 17 or 18 could be tallied twice.

The statistical data for the 1830 and 1840 censuses follow a similar pattern, but with more subdivisions. This was conveniently accomodated by forming two rows with the male data on the upper row, and the female, slave and free colored data on the lower row. The age categories are: under 5, 5 to 10, 10 to 15, 15 to 20, 20 to 30, 30 to 40, 40 to 50, 50 to 60, 60 to 70, 70 to 80, 80 to 90, 90 to 100, and over 100.

Since the format used allows only one character per column, numbers greater than 9 are represented by upper and lower case letters of the alphabet as follows:

A	10	N	23	a	36	n	49
B	11	O	24	b	37	o	50
C	12	P	25	c	38	p	51
D	13	Q	26	d	39	q	52
E	14	R	27	e	40	r	53
F	15	S	28	f	41	s	54
G	16	T	29	g	42	t	55
H	17	U	30	h	43	u	56
I	18	V	31	i	44	v	57
J	19	W	32	j	45	w	58
K	20	X	33	k	46	x	59
L	21	Y	34	l	47	y	60
M	22	Z	35	m	48	z	61

Names, and abbreviations for names, were copied as shown,
even when obviously misspelled; the titles "Jr" and "Sr" were
standardized, however. The researcher who follows a particular
family through the censuses should be tolerant of spelling varia-
tions. As an example, the name GONCE in 1820 was spelled GAUNCE
in 1830 and GONCE again in 1840; SOWSBY was sometimed rendered
SOSBEE, etc.

No townships or household numbers are shown in these censuses, so all names in each census have been arranged in alpha-
betical order to facilitate their use. However, the town of
Carlisle was separately enumerated in 1840. Households in that
town are indicated by an asterisk placed after the name of the
head of the household.

Name	Census		Name	Census
ALEXANDER Jesse	3--2- 1--1- - -		BOYD John	221-1 31-1- - -
ALEXANDER Tho	-11-- 1-1-- - -		BRADLEY Daniel	2--1- 1-1-- - -
ALLEN John	1-2-- --131 - -		BRADLEY George	3-21- 1--1- - -
ALLEN William	21-1- 1-1-- - -		BRADLEY Robt	11-1- 2--1- - -
ALLEN William	2--1- 1--1- - -		BRADSHAW David	1-1-1 11--1 - -
ALLFROY James	21--1 -11-1 - -		BRENSON John	--1-- --1-- - -
ALLISON Alexr	1--1- 51111 - -		BRENSON Thos	121-2 --21- - -
ALLISON John	3--1- 33-1- - -		BRENTON Eliza	312-- -22-1 - -
ANDERSON Danel	3--1- 111-- - -		BRENTON James	--1-- 1-1-- - -
ANDERSON Edward	31-1- 4-11- - -		BRENTON John	1--1- 2-1-- - -
ANDERSON George	1-2-- 2-1-- - -		BROHS Hanah	----- 2--1- - -
ANDERSON John	3-11- 1311- - -		BROOKS Zach	2--1- 1--1- - 3
ANDERSON Sarah	22--4 1---1 - -		BROWN James	422-1 1111- - -
ARCHER James	---1- --1-- - -		BROWN James	---1- -1-11 - -
ARCHER John	-1-11 --2-1 - 1		BROWN John	----1 ----1 - -
ARCHER Sampson	1--1- 2--1- - -		BROWN John	1--2- 1--1- - -
ARDRY James	-1-11 2-2-1 - -		BROWN John	112-1 21-1- - 2
ARDRY Robt	--1-- --1-- - -		BROWN Parker	1--1- 2-1-- - -
ARMSTRONG Irvin	1-1-- 1-1-- - -		BROWN Wm	22-1- 1-11- - -
ARNOLD H Lewis	2--1- 1-1-- - -		BUCHANAN Phebe	-1--- ----1 - B
ARNTT Samuel	3--1- 12-1- - 6		BUCKLEAR Stephen	12--1 21-1- - -
ART William	--111 ----1 - -		BUCKNER Henry	1-2-- 1-1-- - 5
ART William Jr	--1-- 2-1-- - -		BUCKNER Saml	---1- ----- - 5
ASBURY Henry	--3-1 --3-1 - 4		BUNTON Andrew	3--2- 1--1- - -
ASBURY William	2---1 -1-11 - 6		BUNTON James	1--1- 3---- - -
ASBURY William	3--1- ---11 - 7		BUNTON William	1111- 2--11 - -
ASHCRAFT Jacob	231-1 41-1- - -		BURDEN Chas	31--1 -111- - -
ASHCROFT Ephraim	-2-1- 22-1- - -		BURNETT Wm	111-2 2121- - -
BAILEY Basil	211-1 42-1- - -		BURNS John	-2-1- -111- - -
BAILEY John	32-1- 1--1- - -		BURNS John	2--1- ---1- - -
BAKER Jacob	32-1- 1211- - -		BURRESS John	32-1- 1--1- - -
BAKER James	1--1- 4111- - -		BURTON Josiah	-1211 -1111 - -
BAKER John	1--1- 1-1-- - 3		BUSBY Matthew	215-1 --1-1 - -
BAKER John	----1 ----1 - -		BUSBY William	21-1- 1111- - -
BAKER Martin	1-1-1 ----1 - 3		BYERS David	211-1 -331- - -
BAKER Wm	1--1- 22-1- - 6		BYERS john	1-1-- --1-- - -
BALLENGER Wm	42--1 1-11- - -		BYRAM Augustin	2--1- 1-1-- - 1
BALLINGAL David	2-111 2111- 1 2		CALDWELL Alexr	--1-1 ----1 - -
BARLOW Jesse	4--1- --1-2 - -		CALDWELL David	1--1- 1----- - -
BARLOW John	52-1- 2--1- - -		CALDWELL David	-1-1- 121-1 - -
BARLOW Wm	1231- 11-1- - 1		CALDWELL Robt	111-1 212-1 - -
BARNETT Ambrose	111-1 11--1 - -		CALDWELL Robt	2--1- 2--1- - -
BARNETT John	1--1- --1-- - -		CALDWELL Robt	--1-- --1-- - -
BARTLETT Ebenezar	--21- 4--1- - -		CALDWELL Thos	2--1- 2--1- - -
BARTLETT Joseph	--2-- --1-- - -		CALDWELL Thos	2--1- 2--1- - -
BARTLETT Saml	21-1- 2--1- - -		CALDWELL Walter	3111- -1-1- - 5
BARTLETT Wm	-11-1 -2-11 - 1		CALDWELL Wm	212-1 3111- - -
BASNETT Jesse	22-1- 11-1- - 6		CALDWELL Wm	----1 ----1 - -
BEATON John	2---1 21--1 - -		CAMPBELL Daniel	3--1- 21-1- - -
BEDINGER G N	321-1 1111- - F		CAMPBELL James	231-1 ---1- - -
BELL Jane	112-- -211- - -		CAMPBELL John	2--1- --1-- - -
BELL Jane	11--- ----1 - -		CAMPBELL Josius	2--11 1221- - -
BENINGTON Nelson	2---1 21-1- - -		CAMSON Samuel	-1111 -11-1 - -
BENTLY Michael	1221- 11-1- - -		CARNAHAN James	-1--1 ----1 - -
BEREY Robert	2111- 322-- - 5		CARNAHAN James	2--1- 1--1- - -
BLACKBURN H	--1-- --1-- - -		CARNAHAN Robert	2--1- 1-2-- - -
BLAIR Alexr	-24-1 111-1 - -		CARNS Adam	-211- 213-1 - -
BLAIR Sarah	1---- 1121- - -		CARTER Daniel	34-1- 1--1- - -
BLASTINGEM Wm	---1- ----- - -		CARTER Johnathan	2--1- ---1- - -
BOATMAN Henry	12--1 ---1- - -		CARUTHERS Thos	--3-1 ---1- - 1
BOGGAS Thos	-11-1 2111- - 3		CASADAY Danel	21-11 1-11- - -
BOLES John	2-1-1 22-1- - -		CASADAY James	31-1- 2--1- - -
BOLES William	1-11- --1-1 - -		CASADAY Jessy	---2- 2-21- - -
BOSLEY Benard	42--1 11-1- - -		CASESEY James	21-1- 2--1- - -
BOWEN Wm	3--1- 1131- - -		CASESEY John	22--1 22--1 - -
BOYD John	2--1- 1-11- - -		CASSOGOUGH Peter	212-1 212-1 - -

Name	Col 1	Col 2	Name	Col 3	Col 4
CATHERWOOD Chas	-1111	-22-1 - -	DUNCAN William	--1-1	121-1 - 3
CATHERWOOD Saml	32--1	2111- - -	EARLIWINE Danl	21--1	23-1- - -
CAUGHEY David	--1--	---1- - -	EARLIWINE George	1-11	121-1 - 1
CAUGHEY John	--3-1	-11-1 - -	EARLIWINE Jacob	--1--	--1-- - -
CHANEY James	---1-	--1-? - 1	EASLY Joseph	--1--	2-1-- - -
CHANEY John	-23-1	-1-2- - 3	EASTUS Thos	31-11	11-11 1 1
CHANEY Wm	1---1	2--1- - 3	EATON Jacob	41--1	1221- - -
CHEANEY John	2--1-	2--1- - -	EAVENS John	21-1-	31-1- - -
CLARK Benjamin	--211	-322- - Y	EAVENS Rachel	-1-1-	---1-- - -
CLARK Benjm	--1--	2-1-- - -	EDWARDS Hannah	-1-1-	--11- - -
CLARK David	11-1-	--11- - -	ELLERBECK Jos	---1-	--1-- - -
CLARK John	311-1	-2211 - -	ELLIS James	--1--	2-1-- - -
CLARK William	32--1	2--11 - -	ELLIS James	--411	-12-1 - -
CLAY William	-22-1	----1 - 6	ELLIS John	1-11-	1--1-- - -
COCHRAN Margaret	1----	22-1- - -	FARMER Chas	2111-	3--1-- - -
COLLIER Claborne	2--1-	1-1-- - 2	FEARMAN John	1--1-	3--1-- - -
COLLIER Coleman	--1--	------ - 1	FEEBACK Fred	112-1	111-1 - -
COLLIER Hamlet	1--1-	3--1- - 4	FERN Hugh	2-1-1	143-1 - -
COLLIER John	1--21	-12-1 - J	FIELD Ebanezar	3--1-	42-1- - 1
COLLINS Edmund	1-11-	411-- - 1	FIELD William	2--1-	2--1-- - -
COLLINS Stephen	2--1-	2--1- - 2	FIELDER George	-21-1	3-11- - A
CONWAY John	-23-1	-1-2- - 3	FITE Jacob	1--1-	1--1-- - -
COOK John	11--1	31--1 - -	FITZPATRICK James	-1-1	52-1- - -
COOK Peter	--1--	1-1-- - -	FOSTER Harrison	3--1-	2--1-- - -
COOPER John	2121-	21-1- - -	FOSTER Rhode	-----	----1 - -
COOPER John	2121-	21-1- - -	FOUTH John	12--1	121-1 - -
CORBIN Abraham	21-1-	2--1- - 3	FOWLER James	----1	----1 - -
CORD Asbury	1-11-	--2-1 - -	FRAZIER James	12-1-	2-1-- - -
COSBY Overton	111--	1-1-1 - -	FRAZIER William	----1	----1 - -
COTREL Thos	1---1	211-1 - -	FRY John	--1--	--1-- - -
COWEN Isaac	11-1-	22-1- - -	FRYMAN Henry	--1--	--1-- - -
CRAWFORD Sam	1--1-	--2-1 - -	FRYMAN Philip	-1--1	-1--1 - -
CRAWFORD William	1-1--	1-1-- - -	FULLER Joseph	--1--	--1-- - -
CULP Thos	--1--	1-1-- - 1	FULTON Samuel	1-11-	--11- - -
DAILY John	---1-	111-- - -	GADMAN William	1-1--	--1-- - -
DAILY Mary	-----	--1-1 - 2	GADSEY Gilbert	1--1-	1-1-- - -
DARLING Abraham	--1-1	2-11- - -	GAHIL Holly	22---	----1 - -
DARROW James	21-1-	1-1-- - -	GALBREATH Ben	1-1-1	--1--- - -
DAVIDSON John	-1--1	--1-1 - 1	GALBREATH Wm	11--1	2111- - -
DAVIDSON John Jun	--1--	--1-1 - -	GILLASPY James	1-11-	1--1-- - -
DAVIS Robert	1-1-1	-21-1 - -	GITHENS Henry	21-1-	2--1-- - -
DAVIS Thomas	---1-	2-1-- - -	GITHENS James	----1	----1-- - -
DAVIS Thomas	111-1	11-1- - -	GITHENS John	1--1-	--1--- - -
DAVIS William	2-31-	--1-- - 1	GLASCOCK Cena	-----	1--1-- - -
DAYTON Garrett	1-111	221-1 - -	GLASCOCK Peggy	-----	1--1-- - -
DEEN Abraham	33--1	----1 - -	GLEN Simeon	---1-	--1-- - 1
DEWITT Henry	--2-1	--11- - -	GOGHAGAN John	--1--	2-1-- - 1
DICKEY Alexander	1-1--	1-1-- - 1	GOGHAGAN John	----1	121-1 - -
DILL Abner	-11--	2-1-- - -	GONCE George	13-1-	4--1-- - -
DILL Matthew	431-1	--11- - 3	GONCE Nicholas	--1-1	----1 - -
DINGLE William	4--1-	1-1-- - 1	GORMAN Danl	---1-	1--1-- - -
DINSMORE Henry	----1	----2 - -	GRAGG Joseph	---1-	1-1-- - -
DINSMORE John	212-1	2221- - -	GRAHAM James	3---1	11-1- - 1
DOSAN Jacob	----1	1--1-- - -	GRAY David	31-1-	1-11- - -
DOSAN William	1--1-	1--1-- - -	GRAY David	3111-	2111- - -
DOTSON James	12-1-	-1-1- - -	GRAY Isaac	21-1-	--1-- - -
DOUGHTERY Jiss	---1-	--1-- - 1	GRAY James	--1--	--1-- - -
DOUGHTERY John	---1-	--1-- - -	GRIFFIN Gabriel	2--1-	3--11 - -
DOUGHTERY Thos	-1--1	--1-- - -	GRIFFITH Martin	2--1-	1--1- - 1
DOUGHTY John	1--1-	2--1-- - -	GROSVENOR Richd	-11-1	1---1 - -
DOUGHTY William	1-11-	1-2-- - -	GUNSANLUS James	-1--1	231-1 - -
DOWNEY Archd	31-1-	21-1- - -	GUNSANLUS Thos	1-3--	1-2-- - -
DRUMMOND James	12--1	1-1-1 - -	HALL Benjamin	322-1	11--1 - -
DUNCAN Archb	4211-	-111- - 3	HALL Cornelius	3--1-	22-1- - 7
DUNCAN James	---1-	2-1-- - -	HALL James	121-1	11--1 - 4
DUNCAN Joseph	1---1	-1---- - 7	HALL Moses	111-1	21--1 - 2

Name	Census	Name	Census
HALL Robert	3--1- 1--1- - -	KEITH Jacob	3211- 2-11- - -
HALL Samuel	---1- 1-1-- - 1	KEITH Philip	3211- 3121- - -
HALL William	-111- --211 - -	KELLEY Thomas	11--1 111-1 - -
HAMILTON John	213-1 12-1- - -	KENADAY Audry	1--1- 2--1- - -
HAMILTON Thos	--1-1 3311- - 1	KENADAY David	14--1 5-21- - -
HANES George	21-1- 2--1- - -	KENADAY Robert	2--1- 2--11 - -
HANSEN Jacob	31--1 -1-1- - -	KILGOUR William	3--1- 3--1- - -
HARBERT Wm	-3--1 --1-1 - -	KIMBROUGH Eliza	21--- 1111- - -
HARDEN Elihu	--1-1 -12-1 - -	KIMBROUGH John	--1-- ----- - 4
HARDEN John	1--1- --1-- - 3	KIMBROUGH Richard	---1- 2--1- - -
HARNEY Mills	121-1 -2-1- - -	KIMBROUGH Robert	--1-- ----- - -
HARNEY Roland	---1- ---1- - -	KINCART James	2--1- 12-1- - -
HARNEY Thos	---1- 1-1-- - -	KINCART John	-21-1 11-1- - -
HARTLEY Eliza	2111- 12-1- - -	KINCART Samuel	--2-1 -2--1 - -
HARTROCK Saml	1111- 1--1- - -	KING Barnett	--1-- ----- - -
HASLET Samuel	2--1- 2--1- - -	KRUSOR Michael	2--1- 41-1- - -
HAWKINS Saml	1-11- 4321- - -	LILLY Pleasant	1--1- 2-1-- - 1
HAWKINS Thos	212-1 111-1 - -	LIVENGOOD George	3--1- 2-11- - -
HEDLETON Alen	31-1- 11211 - -	LOCKRIDGE James	--1-- --1-- - -
HELPMAN John	----1 ----- - -	LOCKRIDGE John	--2-1 --1-1 - -
HENRY John	13111 --11- - -	LOCKRIDGE William	4--1- 411-1 - -
HILDRETH Squire	21-1- 22-1- - -	LOGAN David	31111 2111- - -
HILL James	2-11- 52-1- - -	LONG Samuel	2--1- 1--1- - -
HILL John	3--1- 32-11 - -	LOUDERBACK Andy	31--1 1121- - -
HILLOCK Alex	--111 -11-- - 1	LOW Isaac	2-1-1 4-21- - -
HINTON Ezekiel	2--1- 43-1- - -	LOWE George	21-1- 31-1- - -
HITCH Wiseman	3--1- 11-1- - 3	LUKER John	----1 --2-1 - 2
HOLLADAY Wm	22--1 3--11 - -	MADDEN Susan	-1--- ---1- - -
HOLLAR Francis	2--1- ---1- - -	MAFFIT Henry	1--2- 1-1-- - -
HOLLEY Thompson	1--1- 3111- - 8	MAFFIT Thos	2-21- 2--11 - 2
HOSEN Majhor	2--1- 12-1- - -	MAFFIT Wm	---1- 1-1-- - 1
HOWARD Gideon	-13-1 --1-1 - -	MANIR Meredith	1211- 2-11- - -
HOWARD Gideon	1-1-- --1-- - -	MANIR Samuel	3--1- ---1- - -
HOWARD Henry	1-1-- 2-1-- - -	MANN Jacob	12-1- 3--1- - -
HOWARD Jacob	3--1- 4--1- - -	MANN John	31-1- 34-1? - -
HOWE Samuel	221-1 11--1 - -	MANN Peter	3--1- 1-11- - 1
HOWERTON George	2--1- -2-11 - -	MARELL Wm	121-1 111-1 - -
HUFMAN Peter	--111 1-1-1 - -	MARSH John	21-1- 21-1- - -
HUGHES Wm	241-1 --1-1 - -	MARSH Thos	4--11 2221- - 8
HUNTER John	12-1- 2--1- - -	MARSHALL Archd	1-1-1 3121- - 1
HYATT Shedrick	4--1- 1-1-- - -	MARSHALL David	2--1- ---11 - -
HYRAM Harvey	3--1- ---1- - -	MARSHALL Hugh	1-1-- 2-1-- - -
INGLES Peter	4--1- 1--1- - -	MARSHALL Ralph	-11-1 --1-1 - -
INLOW Jesse	4--1- 23-1- - 3	MARSHALL Saml	2--1- 2--1- - -
INSTEITH Joseph	12111 41-1- - -	MARSHALL Thos	--1-- --1-- - -
IRVEN Andrew	-13-1 --1-1 - -	MARTIN James	2--1- --1-- - -
IRVIN George	1-1-- --1-- - -	MARTIN John	211-2 21--1 - -
ISHMAEL John	--1-- --1-- - -	MARTIN Micah	2--1- 2-1-- - -
ISHMAEL Thomas	2-11- 1-1-- - -	MASON Burges	----1 -1--1 - 9
JETT James	11-1- 1-1-- - -	MATHERS Given	1--1- 1-1-- - -
JOHNSON Isam	4--1- 2-1-- - 9	MATHERS James	1-1-- --1-- - -
JOHNSON James	---1- 1-11- - -	MATHERS William	1-1-- 11-11 - -
JOHNSON James	3--1- -1-1- - -	MATHERS Wm	-22-1 -1-11 - -
JOHNSON John	4--1- 1--1- - -	MAYNOR Jesse	2--1- --11- - -
JOHNSON John	1---1 ---1- - -	MEACH Alexr	2--1- 2--1- - -
JOHNSON Johnathan	3311- 11-1- - -	MEREDITH Abs	1--1- 3--1- - -
JOHNSON Mason	-1--1 -1--1 - -	METCALF Eli	5112- 2111- - 5
JOHNSON Wm	3111- 1--1- - 3	METCALF Thos	2-21- 1-2-1 - 8
JOLLEY David	221-1 4121- - -	MILLER Abram	-1--1 21-11 - -
JONES Drury	---1- 1-1-- - -	MILLER James	---1- 1-1-- - -
JONES Jacob	--211 --111 - -	MITCHELL Ezekiel	----1 ----- - -
JONES John	1-21- --2-- - -	MOLER Isaac	3--1- 3--1- - -
JONES Moses	1--1- 51-11 - A	MONICAL Chester	212-1 -11-1 - -
JUVENALL David	1--1- 41-1- - 1	MONICAL George	21-1- 1111- - -
JINKINS Mary	111-- 1-11- - -	MONICAL Peter	21-1- 11-11 - -
KEITH Adam	12-1- 3--1- - -	MOOR John	3--1- 1-1-- - 1

Name	Tally
MOOR Simun	----1 ------ - -
MORGAN Agnes	1--11 1--1- - -
MORGAN Chas	211-1 2111- - -
MORGAN Garrett	31-1- 1--1- - -
MORRIS Morris	2--1- --1-- - -
MORRIS Thos	3---1 31-1- - -
MULLEN Samuel	1-1-- --1-- - -
MUNSON Joel	1-1-- --1-- - -
MURPHY W George	2--1- 1-1-- - -
MURPHY Zeph	11--1 -1311 - -
MYERS David	1--1- 1-1-- - -
MYERS John	1223- 31-1- - 1
MYERS Margaret	-15-- -22-1 - -
McALL James	2-111 312-1 - -
McCABE James	1-1-- ----- - -
McCABE Jorins	2-11- -111- - 4
McCABE William	-11-1 --1-1 - 1
McCALL John	1-3-- --1-- - -
McCALL Wm	3--1- 1--1- - -
McCANAHAN Archd	1-11- 3--1- - -
McCANAHAN James	11212 2--11 - 1
McCANAHAN John	2--1- 1--1- - -
McCANAHAN William	2-11- 2--1- - -
McCARTY David	-13-1 -1-11 - -
McCARTY Thos	3--1- 2--1- - -
McCLAIN Chas	-1--1 212-1 - -
McCLINTOCK Hugh	31--1 11--1 - -
McCLINTOCK Jos	113-1 -21-1 - -
McCLINTOCK Jos	3-32- 2-11- - -
McCLURGH Jas	53-1- --11- - -
McCORD David	211-1 1111- - -
McCORD John	---1- 1-1-- - -
McCORD Michel	4--1- 21-11 - -
McCORD William	51--1 -1111 - -
McCORMACK Adam	2-21- 4--1- - 3
McCORMACK Eliza	113-- 1-2-1 - -
McCOWN Lawrence	22-1- 1111- - -
McCOY Daniel	1-1-1 12--- - -
McCUNE John	113-1 111-1 - -
McCUNE Robert	21-11 21-21 - -
McCUNE Robert	22211 11--1 - -
McDONALD Alexr	2--1- 1-1-- - -
McDONALD Alexr	3-21- 1-11- - -
McDONALD George	11211 1-1-1 - -
McDONALD John	1-1-- --1-- - -
McDONALD Jos	----1 -2--1 - -
McDONALD Mary	----- 5--1- - -
McDONALD Mordica	12-1- 2121- - -
McFARLAND Wm	132-1 21-11 - -
McGINIS William	22-1- 21-1- - -
McGLOLAN John	--2-- ----- - -
McGLOLAN John	--1-1 --11- - -
McGUIRE John	---1- ----- - -
McMAHAN Robert	22--1 3--1- - -
McMANICE Christo	----1 --1-- - 3
McMEHAN Danl	--12- ----- - -
McNALTY James	--1-- 1-2-- - -
McNALTY Joseph	1---1 121-1 - -
NESBIT Nathan	1---1 1111- - -
NESBIT Thos	31-1- 1121- - -
NESBIT Thos	1---1 1111- - -
NEVVES Daniel	131-1 2--1- - -
NEWDIGATE John	--1-- 1-2-- - -
NEWDIGATE Wm	----1 ----1 - -
NICHUL Robt	11-1- 21-1- - -
NILSON Moris	---1- 1--1- - -
OGDON Mary	----- --1-1 - -
OLANAN Susan	1---- 11--1 - -
OLLIVER John	--1-1 -1--1 - -
OLLIVER Thos	--21- --1-- - -
OVERBY Henry	1--1- 1--1- - -
OVERFIELD Moses	1--1- 2-2-- - -
PADGETT Daniel	1--1- --1-- - -
PARKS James	--1-- 1-1-- - -
PARKS James	1--1- 1-1-- - -
PARSONS John	422-1 2111- - -
PATTON Stephen	21-1- 31-1- - -
PAXTON Robert	22-1- 21--1 - -
PAYTON Sam	222-2 1-211 - -
PAYTON Stephen	2-1-- --1-- - -
PAYTON Stephen	2-1-- --1-- - -
PAYTON Thos	212-1 --1-- - -
PECKERER Nancy	2---- 2--1- - -
PENDERGRASS Edwin	3---1 -4-1- - -
PHILLIPS Bernard	2--1- 1--1- - -
PHILLIPS Joshua	1--1- 1-1-- - -
PLEUGH Elias	1-1-1 -12-1 - -
PLEUGH Jessy	13-1- 3--1- - -
POISAL Jessy	32--1 2--1- - -
POTS Fred	--41- 2-2-- - 1
POTS John	---1- --1-- - -
POTS Samuel	--1-- --1-- - -
POTTS William	12111 -1-1- - 8
POWEL George	1-1-- 1-2-- - -
POWEL Jessy	---1- 1-1-- - -
POWEL John	2--1- 1-1-- - -
POWEL Thos	-1-11 ----1 - -
POWEL Thos	1--1- 2-1-- - -
POWEL Zinns	41-1- 21-1- - -
POWELL Charles	2--1- 3--1- - -
POWER Wiliam	3--1- 11-1- - -
POWLY John	-141- ----1 - -
PRATHER Ashford	--1-- --1-- - -
PRATHER Jessy	1--1- 2-11- - -
PRATHER Jessy Sr	---11 ---1- - 4
PRITCHETT Wm	----1 113-1 - 6
PURCELL Thos	2--1- 2--1- - -
PURNELL Wm	---1- ---1- - 1
RAMSEY Archd	2---1 3211- - -
RANKINS Moses	21-1- 3--1- - -
RAY Francis	-12-1 212-1 - -
REDDING Eli	2--1- --1-- - -
REDDING Wm	3-11- 1-1-- - -
RETZEL Peter	12-1- ---1- - -
REVEAL Joseph	1232- -2-1- - -
REVEAL Michael	----1 --1-1 - -
REVEAL Thos	4--1- 1--1- - -
RHODES Buchn	111-1 22421 - -
RILEY John	1-1-1 3221- - -
RITCHEY Sollom	3--1- 1-2-- - -
RITCHEY Esau	2-1-- 2-1-- - -
RITCHEY Gelbert	-21-- 1--11 - -
RITCHEY Isaac	12--1 2-11- - -
RITCHEY Noah	--1-- 1-1-- - -
RITCHEY Robert	121-1 2-1-1 - -
RITCHEY Wm	2--1- 2-1-- - -
ROBERTS Henly	61-1- 2-11- - -
ROBERTS Hez	313-1 1111- - -
ROBERTS John	--1-- --1-- - -
ROBERTS Nelson	----1 ----1 - -
ROBERTS Thos	44-1- 1-1-- - -
ROBERTSON Alexr	1---1 ---1- - -

Name	Census	Name	Census
ROBERTSON James	----1 ----1 - 2	SWART James	31-11 11-1- - -
ROBERTSON Sam	1121- 112-1 - -	TAYLOR George	2--1 1--1- - -
ROSS Allexander	2-2-- -3--1 - -	TAYLOR George	---1 --1-- - -
ROZIER Adam	2--1 2-2-- - -	TAYLOR Joshua	----1 ----1 - 3
RUNELS Nich	1-3-- 1-1-- - -	TAYLOR Nat	--1-1 ----1 - j
SADLER Edward	--1-- ----- - -	THOMA Edward	21-1 3111- 1 -
SADLER John	1--1 31-1- - -	THOMPKINS Nat	1--1 3-1-- - -
SAMPLE Mary	1---- 12-1- - -	THOMPSON Alexr	11-1 1--1- - -
SANDERS Clem	-4--1 31-1- - -	THOMPSON Henry	---11 -1--- - 2
SANDERS Hish	2----1 2211- - -	THOMPSON James	4--11 -1-11 - -
SANDERSON John	3--1 2-1-- - -	THOMPSON Sally	----- 11-1- - 2
SANDERSON Mary	----- --1-1 - -	THOMPSON Samuel	1--1 -1--- - -
SANDERSON Robt	1--1 --1-- - -	THOMPSON Wm	-23-1 --1-1 - -
SAVATIER Wm	----1 ----1 - -	THORNTON Audery	--3-1 --2-1 - -
SCOTT Andrew	2--1- --2-- - -	THROCKMORTON A	--1-- ----- - 5
SCOTT John	11-1 1-1-- - -	THROCKMORTON John	2--1 1-1-- - 7
SCOTT Matthew	1--1 1-1-1 - -	THROCKMORTON Thos	----1 ----- - 6
SCOTT Thomas	4-11- 2--1 - -	TOWLER luke	1---- 1--1- - 5
SCOTT Thomas	22-1 4--1- - -	TRULOVE C Will	--1-- --2-- - -
SCOTT Thos	----1 ----- - -	UNGLES John	-1-1 3--1- - -
SEERS John	12-1 221-1 - 3	VANHOOK Abner	1--1 --1-- - -
SELBY Isaac	1--1 1--1- - 1	VANHOOK Arch	3--1 3--1- - -
SHANAN Margaret	122-- -11-1 - -	VANHOOK Sam	-1-11 --1-1 - -
SHANKLAND Dan	21-1 ---1- - -	VANSCOTH Hiza	2--1 2111- - -
SHANKLAND John	22--1 --2-1 - -	VAUGHN Thos	-1--1 -1-1- - 4
SHANON john	12-1 1-1-- - -	VERDIN Hugh	----1 3-11- - -
SHARP T John	23-1 1--1- - -	VERNOZ Frances	23-11 ----1 - 2
SHORT George	1-1-- --1-- - -	WAGGONER Charles	-2-1 51-1- - -
SLOOP Joseph	22--1 1---1 - -	WAGGONER John	31-1 2--1- - -
SMALLEY John	--1-- --1-- - -	WALLACE Wm	221-1 --11- - -
SMITH Abram	--1-- 3--1- - -	WARREN Isaac	1--1 21-1- - -
SMITH David	-1-1- 1-1-- - -	WATES Charles	---1- --1-- - -
SMITH Hezch	4---1 13-1- - -	WATES John	31-1 3--1- - -
SMITH Hugh	1-1-- 1-1-- - -	WATSON James	---11 --31- - -
SMITH Jas	31--1 222-1 - -	WATSON James	---1 3--1- - -
SMITH John	--1-- 1-1-- - -	WAUGH Jacob	1-11 3211- - -
SMITH Mitchel	---1- ----- - -	WAUGH Jacob	41-1 1121- - 1
SMITH William	--121 -121- - -	WEBB Charles	2-11 11-1- - -
SNAP George	1--2 3--1- - -	WEBSTER Nath	-12-- 1-1-- - 1
SNAP Peter	222-1 --2-1 - -	WEST Amos	1--1 32-1- - 4
SNAP Samuel	--1-- --1-- - -	WEST Isaac	-11-1 -11-1 - -
SPAUGH Henry	--12 31-1- - -	WEST Phillip	1-1-- --1-- - -
SPAUGH Jacob	3--1 1--1- - -	WEST Thomas	311-1 2111- - 1
STANDIFORD Azn	2--1 2--1- - -	WEST Thomas	1-2-- --2-- - -
STANDIFORD George	1--1 2-1-- - -	WEST john	3--1 1-1-- - -
STANDIFORD Sarah	--1-- --1-1 - 8	WHEELER Wm	31-1 1211- - -
STEPHENSON Robt	1-1-- --1-- - -	WHITE John	22--1 211-1 - -
STEPHENSON Elija	112-- 1-1-1 - -	WHITELY Wm	1-1-- --11- - -
STEPHENSON Jos	1-1-- 1--2- - -	WHITIKER James	1--1 2-1-- - 1
STEPHENSON Robt	3--1 11-1- - -	WHITTLEY Danl	4--1 1--1- - -
STEPHENSON Thos	212-1 212-1 - -	WIGGINS John	22--1 --1-1 - 3
STEVENSON Wm	-32-1 1-1-1 - -	WIGGINS Wm	--1-- --1-- - -
STEWART Jos	5111- -2-1 - -	WILEY Hugh	---2- 3-1-- - -
STEWART Mary	-1--- 11-1- - -	WILEY John	--1-1 1---1 - -
STEWART Williby	2--1 42-1- - -	WILEY John Jur	---1 2--1- - -
STOCKWELL John	-121 1-1-- - 2	WILEY Samuel	1--1 3111- - -
STOGDALE James	-12-1 -1-1- - -	WILLIAMS John	2--1 12-1- - -
STOGDALE Wm	2--1 2--1 - -	WILLIAMS Wm	1--1 2--1- - -
STOOPS Phillip	31-1- --22-1 - -	WILLIAMSON John	1--1 1--1- - -
SUMERVEAL Nicha	2--1 22-1- - -	WILLS Aaron	4---1 2411- - -
SUMMETT Charles	----1 1---1 - -	WILLS Bavia	---1 42-1- - -
SUMMETT George	-22-1 231-1 - -	WILLS Nathan	--1-- --1-- - -
SUTER John	2--1- --1-- - 1	WILLS John	32-1 1--1- - -
SUTTON Ebenezar	----1 -1-1- - -	WILSON Ben	--1-1 --2-1 - -
SWAIN Nathan	2--1 21-1- - -	WILSON Isaac	3--1 1--1- - -
SWANSON John	-1--1 21-1- - -	WILSON James	2--1 2-11- - -

WILSON James	4--1- 1--1- - -	YOUNG Jacob	11-1- 52-1- - -
WILSON Jane	----- --1-- - -	_____ Mary	----- ----- 1 -
WOOD Hillby	--1-- ----- - -	_____ Nancy	----- ----- 1 -
WOOLEN Leonard	1--1- 3-1-- - -	_____ Obadiah	----- ----- 2 -
WOOLMS Wm	21-1- 31-1- - -	_____ Pompey	----- ----- 1 -
YATES Andrew	1-111 ----1 - 1	_____ Rachel	----- ----- 1 -
YATES William	----1 -21-1 - -	_____ Sarah	----- ----- 2 -
YOUNG Alexr	3--1- 1--1- - -	_____ Titus	----- ----- 6 -

Name	Tally 1	Tally 2		
ADAIR Benjamin T	31--1-	2211-	-	-
ADAIR Francis	3---1-	11-1-	1	-
ADAIR Richard	2---1-	2-1--	-	-
ADAMS Alexr	----1-	3--1-	-	-
ADAMS James	-1-1-	1-1-1	-	-
ADAMS Thomas	22---1	1211-	-	-
AINSWORTH Charles	---1--	--1--	-	-
ALEXANDER James	11-2--	--1--	-	2
ALEXANDER John	11-1--	---1--	-	-
ALEXANDER Randolph	2111-1	2211-	-	-
ALEXANDER Thomas	2--11-	2-1--	-	-
ALEXANDER Zacheus	41--1-	12-1-	-	-
ALFREY James	---2-1	-1--1	4	2
ALLEN James	1--11-	--12-	-	-
ALLEN Jesse	2---1-	1-1--	-	-
ALLEN John	3---1-	2--1-	-	-
ALLISON John	1211-1	1-31-	-	-
ANDERSON John	-----1	----1	-	-
ANDERSON Sarah	-111--	-1--1	-	-
ANTROBUS Benjamin	----1-	1-1--	-	-
ANTROBUS John	3---1-	1--2-	1	-
ARCHER Elizabeth	------	---11	1	-
ARCHER Sampson	31--1-	12-1-	-	-
ARDEREY James	1---1-	1-1--	-	-
ARDEREY James	----1-	-11-1	-	-
ARDEREY Robert	1---1-	---11	-	-
ARMSTRONG William	---1--	--2--	-	1
ARNETT Saml	21111-	---11	2	8
ARNOLD Lewis H	-2--1-	31-1-	-	-
ASHBROOK Thomas	--12-1	122-1	-	-
ASHCROFT Nimrod	2---1-	1-1--	-	-
ASHLEY James	1--11-	--1--	2	1
ATKINS Thomas B	2---1-	5111-	-	-
BAKER Abraham	---1--	-1---	-	-
BAKER Edmund	---3-1	-221-	-	-
BAKER Isaac	1312-1	2---1	-	-
BAKER Jacob	1---1-	2-1--	-	-
BAKER James	3--11-	2--1-	1	-
BAKER John	21--1-	11-11	-	-
BAKER John	---1--	--1--	-	-
BAKER Joseph	1--1--	--1--	-	-
BAKER Mary	-1----	----1	-	-
BAKER Thomas	----1-	1-2--	-	-
BAKER William	-1---1	111-2	1	-
BALLINGER David	--12-1	-21-2	3	1
BALLINGER Edward	3---11	2-111	1	3
BALLINGER William	-212-1	11--1	1	5
BANISTER Collin	1--1--	--1--	-	-
BANISTER John	1---1-	2-1--	-	-
BANISTER John Sr	---1-1	-2---	-	-
BARLOW John Sr	4---1-	-1---	-	-
BARLOW John Sr	22-2-1	3111-	2	-
BARLOW William	-1-1-1	-1--2	3	6
BARNETT Ambrose	11-2-1	--111	-	-
BARNETT George	1---1-	3--1-	-	-
BARNETT James	-1-1--	2-1--	-	-
BARNETT John	-1---1	-1--1	5	3
BARNETT John	---1--	--1--	-	-
BARNETT John	31--1-	1---1	-	-
BARNETT John Jr	1--1--	--1--	-	-
BARNETT Shenan	2---1-	21-1-	-	-
BARNETT William	3-111-	2111-	-	-
BARNETT William	----1-	2-1--	-	-
BARR Robert	3---1-	1--11	-	-
BARTLETT Haines	---1--	--1--	-	-
BARTLETT Jeffrey	---1--	1-1--	-	-
BARTLETT Samuel	4-111-	-3-1-	-	-
BARTLETT William Sr	--11-1	--1--	2	2
BASIL John	2---1-	42-1-	1	1
BASKETT James	1--1--	--1--	-	-
BASKETT Jesse	-1-1-2	2--1-	3	2
BASKETT John	---1--	--1--	-	1
BASKETT Martin	---11-	--1--	-	-
BEDINGER Daniel	21-21-	3--1-	5	3
BEDINGER George M	11-1-1	1-21-	4	9
BELDING Milly	--11-	----1	-	-
BELL Edward	2---1-	3--1-	-	-
BELL James	1---1-	1--1-	-	-
BELL James	11--1-	2-1--	-	-
BELL Jane	--121-	--1-1	-	-
BELLIS Jacob	1--1--	1-1-1	-	-
BELLIS Philip	1---1-	3--1-	-	-
BENINGTON David	---1--	--1--	-	-
BENINGTON Nehemiah	1--1-1	11-1-	-	-
BERRY Francis	1---1-	311--	-	-
BERRY Joseph	----1-	1-1-1	-	-
BERRY Robert	11-2-1	22-1-	6	2
BERRY Samuel	1---1-	21-1-	-	-
BISHOP Charles H	---1--	1-1--	-	-
BISHOP Daniel	1---1-	1-111	1	-
BISHOP Henry	51--1-	-1-1-	-	-
BISHOP Lemuel	1111-1	-1-11	-	-
BIVENS Noah	---1--	11---	-	-
BLACKBURN Benjamin	1-1--	--1--	-	-
BLACKBURN Julius	1---1-	4--1-	-	-
BLACKBURN Nancy	2-11--	--1-1	-	-
BLAIR Alexander	---211	-3--1	3	-
BLOUNT Andrew	1----1	1-3-1	-	-
BLOUNT Eatha	--12--	-21-1	-	-
BLOUNT Hezekiah	1---1-	2-1--	-	-
BOARDMAN Benjamin	1--3-1	--1-1	-	-
BOARDMAN William	---1--	1-1--	-	-
BOATMAN Henry	--13-1	----1	-	-
BOATMAN William	----1-	21-1-	1	-
BOGGESS Robert	1---1-	2-1--	-	-
BOLES Samuel	2----1	12-1-	-	-
BOND Ealenor	1-----	2--1-	-	-
BOSLEY Benedict	-3-2-1	21--1	-	-
BOULDEN Jesse	----1-	1-1--	-	1
BOWEN William	1112-1	-1--1	-	-
BOWMAN Schadrach	4---1-	---11	-	-
BOYD John Jr	2--1--	--1--	-	-
BOYD John Sr	-112-2	221-1	-	-
BOYD Saml	1-1211	1-1--	-	-
BOYD William	11---1	13111	-	-
BRADLEY George	32--1-	12-1-	-	-
BRADLEY Robert	---1-1	-1--1	-	-
BRADSHAW David	-1---1	----1	-	-
BRADSHAW William	----1-	3-1--	-	-
BRADY Patrick	2-12-1	2211-	-	-
BRANCH Pleasant	--11-1	2-1-1	3	3
BRANHAM Joseph	13-1-1	11--1	-	-
BRECKENRIDGE Polly	-3----	-1-11	-	-
BRENTON Elizabeth	-1131-	--3-1	-	-
BRENTON Robert	----1-	3--1-	-	-
BROOKINGS Vivian	1--1-1	1-1-1	7	6
BROOKS Zachariah	31---1	31-1-	-	2
BROWN Ann	-211--	1---1	-	-
BROWN Beverly	1---1-	2--1-	-	-
BROWN Daniel	3---1-	2-1--	-	-
BROWN John	-----1	----1	-	2
BROWN John	---211	11221	-	-

BROWN Polly	2------ ---1- - -	CARTER John Jr	-1-1-- 1---1 - 1
BROWN Samuel D	1----1- 1111- - -	CASPERELL Edward D	----1- -1-1- - -
BROWN William	1-111- 2--1- - -	CASSEDY Jeremiah	2--112 2--11 - -
BUCHANAN James	1--1-- 3-1-1 3 6	CASSIDY James	21111- -2--1 - -
BUCKLER Robert	2--11- 2--1- - -	CASSITY William	---2-2 1111- 7 3
BUCKLER Stephen	-1-221 12--1 - -	CAUGHEY John	-----1 1-1-1 - -
BUCKNER Henry	11--1- 31-1- 4 5	CAUGHEY Samuel	1--21- --11- - -
BUCKNER Saml	----1- ------ 1 1	CHADWICK Israel	3212-1 -111- 2 4
BUNTON Andrew	22111- --11- - -	CHAMP Robert	----1- 2----- - -
BUNTON James	21---1 3-2-- - -	CHAMP Thomas	311111 21--1 1 1
BUNTON William	23-1-1 2--1- - -	CHANEY William	-1---1 --1-1 3 3
BURCHFIELD Elias	1----1 4--1- - -	CHEANEY John	21-1-1 -111- 3 4
BURDEN Charles	-211-1 --1-1 - -	CHIPLEY John	----1- 2311- - -
BURDEN James	1--1-- 1-1-- - -	CLARKE Jeremiah	42111- --11- - -
BURDEN Saml	2--1-- --1-- - -	CLARKE John	1---1- 1-1-- - -
BURKE George	2---1- -11-- - -	CLARKE Nancy	1---1- ----2 2 2
BURKE James	1---1- --1-- - -	CLARKE Samuel	11-11- -1--1 - -
BURNAW George	1---1- --3-1 - -	CLARKE Singleton	1--1-- 1-1-- - -
BURNS Jacob	1----1 312-- - -	CLARKE Thomas	1-12-- --1-1 - -
BURNS James	2---1- 1--1- - -	CLARKE William	-1-1-1 1-1-- 1 1
BURNS John Jr	3---1- ---1- - -	CLAY William	---2-1 ------ - -
BURNS John Sr	-1-3-1 -1--1 - -	CLAYTON William	----1- 2-1-- - -
BURNS Matthew	1---1- 2-1-- - -	COCKERELL John	11111- 1--1- 5 5
BURNS Robert	---11- 1---1 - -	COLBERT Jesse	12-1-1 111-1 - -
BURNS Saml	1--1-- --1-- - -	COLE John	42--1- 2--1- - -
BURNS William	2-1-1 -311- - 1	COLEMAN Clayton	21-1-- 1-2-- - -
BURTON Josiah	---111 --1-- - -	COLLIER Coleman A	-2--1- 1-1-1 - -
BUSBY Charles	--12-- 1-1-- - -	COLLIER Hamlett	2----1 1211- 5 6
BUSBY Jacob	---1-- --1-- - -	COLLIER Hannah	2----1 11-11 2 1
BUSBY Matthew Jr	2--1-- --1-- - -	COLLIER William	12-2-1 31--1 7 9
BUSBY Matthew Sr	-2--11 -----1 - -	COLLINS Edmund	11---1 33-1- 1 1
BUTLER Joseph D	2---2- 1-1-- - -	COLLINS Thomas	2---1- 11-1- - -
BYERS Elizabeth	12---- ----1 - -	CONWAY John Jr	---2-1 ----2 5 2
BYERS John	-1--1- 3--1- - -	CONWAY William	1---1- --1-1 4 3
BYRAM Augustin	32--1- 31-1- 1 1	CONYERS Azariah	2-112- 2--1- - 1
CALDWELL Alexander	1---11 4-1-- - -	COOK John	-1---1 -11-1 - -
CALDWELL David	1--1-1 1-11- - 1	COOK Martin B	1--11- 1-1-- - 2
CALDWELL David	1--1-- 2-11- - -	COOK Peter	2---1- -1---- - -
CALDWELL David	1----1 1-1-- - -	COOK William	-----1 --3-1 - -
CALDWELL James	---1-- 2-1-- - -	CORBIN Ellin	21-2-- 11-1- 2 3
CALDWELL James	11---1 21-1- - -	COTTINGHAM Isaac	---1-- 1-1-- - -
CALDWELL John	2---1- 1-1-- - -	COTTINGHAM Thomas	2211-1 1111- - -
CALDWELL Joseph	---1-- 2-1-- - -	COTTINGHAM Thomas	12-1-- --11- - -
CALDWELL Robert	22--1- 2-11- - -	COTTINGHAM Wm	2---11 21-1- - -
CALDWELL Robert Sr	---1-1 -21-1 - -	COTTRELL Thomas Jr	----1- 4-1-- - -
CALDWELL Thomas	---1-- 2-1-2 - -	COTTRELL Thomas Jr	1----1 11-11 - -
CALDWELL Thomas	31111- 31-1- - -	COVERDALE Eli	1--1-1 32-1- - -
CALDWELL Thomas	3---11 1--11 - -	COWAN Hugh	111--1 1141- - -
CALDWELL William	--12-1 -23-1 - -	COWAN Isaac	1--2-1 -22-1 - -
CALDWELL William Jr	-----1 3-1-- - -	CRAPPER Laban	23-111 --2-1 - -
CALLOWAY John	21--1- 21-1- - -	CRAWFORD Alexander	1---1- 2--1- - -
CAMPBELL Francis	21--1- 1--1- - -	CRAWFORD John	21--1- 1-2-- - -
CAMPBELL Hugh W	-----1 --1-- 6 2	CRAWFORD Mary	------- ---11 - -
CAMPBELL James	31--1- 3--1- - -	CRAWFORD William	31--1- 11-1- - -
CAMPBELL John	2---1- --1-- - -	CRAY Edward	1--1-- --1-- - -
CAMPBELL John	23---1 3--1- 1 2	CRAY Martin	3---1- --2-- - -
CAMPBELL John	21--1- 1--1- - -	CRESS Valentine	21---1 -1--1 - -
CAMPBELL Joseph	2---1- --1-- - -	CROSE Adam	---1-- 1-1-- - -
CAMPBELL Josiah	1-12-1 111-1 - -	CROSE Andrew	---1-- --1-- - -
CAMPBELL Robert	1--1-1 1-1-- - -	CROUCH David	--12-- 21111 3 1
CAMPBELL Robert	2----1 3--1- - 3	CROUCH Elias	-----1 2--1- - -
CAMPBELL William	1--1-- --1-- - -	CROUCH John	---311 --2-1 - -
CAMPBELL William	1--1-- --1-- - -	CROUCH Johnathan	3----1 1--1- 1 -
CARLIN Joseph	1---1- 2-1-- - -	CROUCH Joseph	2---1- 1--1- - -
CARR James	-1---1 ---1- 3 -	CRUMP Elisha	1---1- 4--1- - 1
CARTER James	21--1- 11-1- - -	CULP Mary	1------ -1-1- - -

CUNNINGHAM Elizabeth	--12-- --2-1 - -	DYER William	--11-1 --1-1 - -
CURTIS Seth	-1-2-1 1-2-- - -	DYKES Robert	---11- 4--1- 2 3
CUSADEN James	----1- 3-2-- - -	EARLYWINE Daniel	---11- 2-1-- - -
DAIZEY Elijah	----2- -2--- 1 1	EARLYWINE George	-----1 --1-1 - -
DALLAS William	----1- -1-1- - -	EARLYWINE Jacob	4---1- 1-1-- - -
DAMPEER Henry	1---1- 4--1- - -	EARLYWINE Mary	-1-1-- 1-2-1 - -
DARROW James	22---1 21-1- - -	EARLYWINE William	1--1-- --1-1 3 1
DARROW John	2---1- 1---1 - -	EARP Simon	22--1- 31-1- - -
DARROW William	2---1- 2-1-- - -	EATON Jacob	1212-1 -1221 - -
DARROW William Sr	---1-1 2--11 - -	EDWARDS Benj	11--1- 221-1 - -
DARSKOCKE Josiah	2---1- 3--1- - -	EDWARDS Robert	---1-- --1-- - 2
DARVILL George	-1-1-1 11-1- - -	ELLIOTT James	3---1- 11-11 - -
DAVIDSON James	---1-- 1-1-1 - -	ELLIOTT John	31--1- 31-1- - -
DAVIDSON John	---1-- 1-2-- - 3	ELLIOTT Robert	1213-1 1111- - -
DAVIDSON John	2---1- 2-1-- - -	ELLIOTT Robert M	----1- -1-1- - -
DAVIDSON Thomas	11-2-1 --1-1 2 2	ELLIS James	----11 --2-1 1 2
DAVIS Alexander	1--1-- --1-- - -	ENDICOTT Joseph	--11-1 432-1 - -
DAVIS James	---1-- --1-- - -	ENLOW Jesse	-3---1 1-2-1 1 3
DAVIS Joshua	----1- --1-- - -	EUBANKS Joseph	1--1-1 211-- 2 5
DAVIS thomas	-1-1-1 61-1- - -	EUBANKS William	1--1-- 1-1-- 1 -
DAZEY Jasper	11--1- 2--1- - -	EVANS Bennett H	2---1- 22-1- - -
DAZEY Johnathan	2---1- -1-1- - 1	EVANS David	21-1-- 12-1- - -
DAZEY Lemuel	-112-1 -1-1- - -	EVANS Gilead	1--11- --1-- - -
DEAL Catherine	12121- 1---1 1 4	EVANS James	2---1- 1-11- - -
DEAL Isaac	2---1- 1-1-- 2 -	EVANS John	-1111- 42-1- - -
DEAN Joseph	---1-- 1-2-- - -	EVANS John	11--1- 3211- - -
DEATLEY Jemima	2122-- ----1 - -	EVANS Michael	1--1-1 122-1 - -
DELANEY John	free color 1 1	FEARMAN Jane	-1---- -121- - -
DELAY Edward	2---1- 32-1- - -	FEEBACK David	4--1-- -211- - -
DELAY john	-----1 --1-1 - -	FEEBACK Gilbert	2--1-- --1-- - 2
DELZELL Abraham	21--1- --1-- - -	FEEBACK Jacob	1---1- 3--1- - -
DELZELL Thomas	---211 -1-12 - -	FEEBACK John	2---1- 1-11- - -
DEVERS John	1---1- 32-1- - -	FEEBACK Mary	3----- ---11 - -
DEVERS Michael	1---1- 3-1-- - -	FIELD Abraham	2---1- 1--1- - -
DEWITT Jacob	1---1- 4---1 1 -	FIELDER George	---2-1 1-2-2 - -
DICKISON Elizabeth	--12-- -1-1- - -	FIELDER John	3---1- 1--1- 3 1
DINGLE William	-1-11- -1-1- - -	FIFER Jacob	21-1-1 2-5-1 - -
DINSDALE Isaac	2---1- --1-- - 1	FIGHT Jacob	41--1- 1--1- - -
DINSMORE Henry	-----1 ----2 - -	FIGHT Jacob	-----1 1--11 - -
DINSMORE Henry	1---2- 11-1- - -	FIGHT John	2---1- 2-1-- - -
DINSMORE John	-1-1-1 -1311 - -	FISHER Zerolabel	2----1 1--11 - -
DONGOON Leonard	22--1- 2--1- - -	FITZPATRICK James	1-2-1 212-1 - -
DONNELL Robert	1--1-- 1-1-- - -	FLEET William	----1- 2--11 1 1
DONNELL Thomas	12-1-1 -11-1 - -	FOLKS Stephen	free color 1 1
DORLAND Abraham	1-2-1 31-1- - -	FORD Robert	2---1- 2--1- - -
DOTSON Daniel	1----1 1-11- - -	FORSYTHE John	2-12-- -11-- - -
DOTSON Dudley	21--1- 22-1- - -	FOSTER David	1--1-- --1-- - -
DOTSON Elijah	1---1- 3--1- - -	FOSTER Henry	21---2 4122- - -
DOTSON James	-----1 ----1 - -	FOSTER James	-----1 --1-1 - -
DOTSON Martin	---1-- 1-1-- - -	FOSTER James Jr	2-1-- -1--- 1 4
DOUGHERTY Jesse	3---1- 2--1- 1 1	FRANKLIN Frederick	2--1-- 1--1- - -
DOUGHTERY John	---3-- --1-- - -	FRANKLIN John	1----1 --1-1 - -
DOUGHTY John	11-2-1 --1-1 1 1	FRY John	2-11- 2-11- - -
DOUGHTY John	1-111- -2-1- - -	FRYMAN George	2---1- 4211- - -
DOUGHTY Skillman	1--1-- 1-1-- - -	FRYMAN Jacob	3---1- 1--1- - -
DOUGHTY Thomas	-----1 ----1 - -	FRYMAN Philip	1----1 -1212 - -
DOUGHTY William	1-111- ---1- - -	FUGATE James Sr	-1-4-1 -1--1 - -
DOWNING Sarah	12-2-- 11-1- - -	FULLER Joseph	3---1- 1--1- - -
DRUMMOND Amos	---1-- 1-1-- - -	FULTON Samuel	3---1- 2--11 - -
DRUMMOND Parker	3--1-- 2--1- - -	GAFFIN Otho	2--11- 2-11- 2 1
DRYDEN Martha	1--1-- 12-1- - -	GEERS Jesse	2-111- 1-11- - -
DUDLEY John	---21- 2-1- 1 1	GEERS John	33--1- ---1- - -
DUNCAN Benjamin	1---1- 2-2-- 2 3	GEOGHAGAN John	-----1 --1-1 2 3
DURAY John	21--1- 3-21- - -	GEOGHEGAN Michael	1---1- 42-1- - -
DURCE Jacob	1---1- --1-- - -	GLASS Thomas J	21--1- 1211- - -
DYE Joseph	----1- 2-1-- - -	GLASSCOCK Abraham	----2- 2--1- - -

Name	Tally
GLENN Simeon	----1- ---1- - -
GODMAN William	2---1- 2---1 2 1
GONCE George	2--1-1 13-1- - -
GONCE John	2---1- 2-1-- - -
GONCE Samuel	---2- --1- - -
GOODRICK Benjamin	4112-1 112-1 - -
GRAFFORT John	31--1 1--1- - -
GRAGG Samuel	-1---1 1--11 - -
GRAVES William	----1- ----1 - 1
GRAY David	2---1 1-1-- - -
GRAY Isaac	21--1 1-11- - -
GRAY James	41111- 1111- - -
GRAY Kitty	31---- 2111- - -
GRAY William	1---1 2-1- - -
GRAY William	1---1- 2--1- - -
GRAYHAM James	---2-1 -11-1 - -
GRIFFITH Thomas	2---1- --1- - -
GRIFFITH Zachariah	11--1 32-1- - -
GRIMES Christian	---1-1 -12-1 - -
GROSSENOR Elizabeth	1----- --1- - -
HAIN Michael Jr	1---1- --1- - -
HALL Benjamin	-112-1 -1--1 - -
HALL Elihu	1---1 2-1- 1 -
HALL Elijah	2--1- 1-1- - 2
HALL Henry	---1- --1- - -
HALL James Jr	1-1- 1-1- - -
HALL James Sr	---1-1 1---1 2 4
HALL Lawrence	--1111 -11-1 - -
HALL Moses Jr	1---1 ---1- 2 2
HALL Moses Jr	--12-1 -11-1 - -
HALL Robert	22--1 111-- - -
HALL Samuel	31--1 21-1- 1 1
HALL William	----2 1--1- 1 -
HALL polly	-111-- ---1- 1 1
HAM Catherine	---11- ----1 - -
HAM Elizabeth	-1-2-- -21-1 - -
HAM Jacob	4---1 1-1-- - -
HAM John Jr	43--1 1--1- - -
HAM Michael	1---1- --1- - -
HAM Samuel	----1- 1-1- - -
HAMILTON Charity	--12-- ----1 1 -
HAMILTON James	1--1- --1- - -
HAMILTON James	1--1- --1- - -
HAMILTON James	2---1- 3-1-- - -
HAMILTON Jason	1---1 2-1- - -
HAMILTON John	1---1- 2-1- - -
HAMILTON John	-2-111 --2-1 2 -
HAMILTON John Sr	21-2-1 212-- - -
HAMILTON Polly	-1-2-- 222-1 - -
HAMILTON Polly	1----- 1--1- - -
HAMILTON Robert	---1-- 111- - -
HAMILTON Samuel	14---1 2-21- - -
HAMILTON William	2---1 ---1- - -
HANNA John	1212-1 --2-1 - -
HANSON Sarah	---2-- -14-1 5 4
HARBERT Henry	1--1- --1- - -
HARBERT John	4---1 1--1- - -
HARBERT John	1---1 3-1-- - -
HARBOUR Thomas	5---1 ---1- - -
HARDY Armstead	1---11 2---1 2 4
HARNEY Hiram	1312-1 2411- - 1
HARNEY Mills	4---1 --1- - -
HARNEY Nancy	1-11-- 2-1-1 - -
HARNEY Rowland	1----1 ---1- - -
HARNEY Thomas	----1- 11-1- - -
HARRIS John	1---1- 2--1- - -
HARRIS John	2312-1 --21- - -
HARRIS Saml	32111- 1--1- - -
HARRIS Titus	free color 3 3
HARTLEY Wiliam	1--1-- --21- - -
HARVEY Samuel A	31--1 1-11- - -
HAWKINS Samuel	-2---1 -1221 - -
HAYDON Mary	1----- --31- 4 3
HAYS John	11--1 2--1- - -
HAYS John	11--2 2211- - -
HEIDELDON Gance	---1-- 113-1 - -
HENDERSON John	3---1 13-1- - -
HENDERSON Robert	1--2-1 32-1- - -
HENDRIX Frederick	31111- 2211- - -
HENDRIX John	21--1 211-- - -
HENLEY James	21--1 3-111 1 1
HENRY George	31--1 21-1- - -
HENRY James	21131- 21-1- - -
HENRY Samuel D	1---1 2-1-- - -
HERNDON Thomas	21-3-1 11-12 - -
HERRINGTON John	22--1 21-1- - -
HIGHLANDER George	----1 1-1-- - -
HILDRETH John	1--1- 1-1- - -
HILDRETH Sarah	31---- 21-21 - 1
HILL Elzy	---1- 1--1- - -
HILL James	3-1111 133-1 - -
HILL John	21-1-1 11211 - -
HILL Otho	2---1 --1- - -
HILL Richard	-1---1 2-1-1 - -
HILLOCK James	3----2 11-1- - -
HINDE Robert	1113-1 111-- - -
HINDMAN William	---1- --1- - -
HINKLE Enoch	---1- 2-1- - -
HINKLE Jane	-1---- -2--1 - -
HINTON Exekiel	-1-11- 232-1 - -
HOGUE William	1---1 2--1- - -
HOLLADAY Thomas	---1- 2-1- 1 -
HOLLADAY William	31---1 111-- 5 6
HOLLER John	22--1 11-1- - -
HOLMES Daniel	1---1 3--1- - -
HOOK Belitha	21111- 2-11- - -
HOOK McKinney	-1-1-1 1-2-- - -
HOOK Thomas	21-211 -2111 - -
HOPKINS George W	42--1 11-1- 1 3
HOPKINS Joseph A	11--1 5--1- 1 1
HOPKINS Josiah	1---1 -1--- - -
HOPKINS Joslin	1--1- ---1- - -
HOPKINS Robert	-111-1 ----1 - -
HOPKINS William	2-12-1 3--1- - -
HOPKINS William	21--1 3-11- - -
HOPKINS john	11--1 -11-1 - -
HORNBACK Adam	1--1-1 -23-1 - -
HOW Jonas	---1-1 ----1 - -
HOW Peter	3---1 31-1- - -
HOW Samuel	5--11 1--1- - -
HOWARD Gideon	3---1 2--1- - -
HOWARD Joshua	2---1 2--1- - -
HOWARD Matthew	2---1 2--1- - -
HOWARD Saml	----1 2--1- - -
HOWARD Thomas	3212-1 11-1- 2 5
HOWE Ann	3---11 ---1- 3 1
HOWE Saml	1112-1 4-111 - -
HOWES Jonathan	---1- --1- - -
HOWES Richard	1---1 3--1- - 1
HUDELSON David	-1-1-1 ---1- - -
HUDELSON James	1---1- 1-1-- - -
HUDELSON William	----11 -12-1 - -

Name	Data		Name	Data
HUDSON Evans	1----1 21-1- - -		LAWSON John	1---1- --1-- - 1
HUDSON Michal	11--1- 11-1- 1 2		LEACH Benjamin	1--1-1 4211- 5 1
HUFFMAN Peter	-----1 -1--1 - -		LEEPER James	2111-1 31211 1 4
HUFFSTUTTER John	11-11- 21-1- - -		LEER Jacob	-----1 --11- 1 2
HUFSTETTER Berry	2---1- 22-1- - -		LETTON Michael	-3---1 113-1 4 2
HUGHES Andrew S	1--11- ---1- - -		LILLY Pleasant	3-11-1 12-1- - -
HUGHES Isaac	31--1- ---2- - -		LINN Timothy	-1-1- 23--1 - -
HUGHES James Jr	12-11- 1122- F A		LIVENGOOD Philip	---1-- 2-1-- - -
HUGHES John	----1- 1-1-- - -		LOCKRIDGE James	2---1- 3--1- - -
HUGHES Toliver	21--1- 3--1- - -		LOCKRIDGE John Sr	----21 1-1-- - -
HUGHES William	-1-2-1 21--1 - -		LOCKRIDGE Robert	-2-11- 51-1- - -
HUGHES William	3---1- 11-2- 4 2		LOCKRIDGE William	2---1- 2131- - -
HUMPHREYS Joseph	12---1 1---1 1 1		LOLLER Robert	-1--1- 2--1- - -
HUNT Israel	-----1 -31-1 - -		LONG Avery	----1- 1--1- - -
HUTSELL Jacob	1---1- 1--1- 3 1		LONG Eliakin	32-1-1 -111- - -
HUTSELL Mathias C	1---1- 2--1- - -		LONG Samuel	22--1- 21-1- - -
HYATT Thomas D	3---1- 1--1- 1 2		LONG Thomas	---1-- 1-1-- - -
IRELAND Thomas	1---1- 2--1- - -		LOUDON John	2---1- -1-1- - -
IRVIN David	3---1- 2--1- - -		LOUDON William	1----1 --1-1 - -
IRVIN John	1---1- 32-1- - -		LOWE Isaac	13---1 -13-1 - -
ISHMAEL Benjamin	---2-1 -1--1 - -		LYNN William	2112-1 4111- - -
ISHMAEL James	31--11 21-1- - -		MADDOX Burnett	22---1 5--1- - -
ISHMAEL John	4---1- 1--1- - -		MADOX Henley	-----1 -13-1 1 2
JAMES Ruth	1--1-- -211- - -		MAGUIR John	-112-1 -1211 - -
JAMESON James	2---1- 2--1- - -		MAGUIR William	12--1- 3--1- - -
JAMESON John	2---1- 311-- - -		MANN Jacob	1--1-- --1-- - 2
JAMESON Samuel J	-----1 --1-1 - -		MANN John	3112-1 222-1 - -
JOHNSON Isham	31---1 2-211 3 5		MANN Peter	32-1-1 --11- - -
JOHNSON James	---1-- --1-- 1 -		MARSHALL Hugh	1---1- 32-1- - -
JOHNSON James	1--1-- --1-- - 1		MARTIN Edmund	1---1- 1-11- - -
JOHNSON Jonathan	1--111 -2-1- - -		MARTIN Jacob	----1- 4-1-- - -
JOHNSON Laban	-1-2-1 -1-1- - -		MARTIN John	-----1 -1--1 - -
JOHNSON Robert	21-11- 131-1 3 2		MARTIN Nehemiah	12--1- 3111- - -
JOHNSON Thomas	2--1-1 123-1 - -		MASTIN Peter	--12-1 ----1 - 1
JOHNSON William	11-2-- 11-1- - -		MATHERS Gavin	21--1- 11-1- - 1
JOHNSON William	32-2-2 ----1 1 -		MATHERS James	1---1- 2-1-- - -
JOLLY James	--13-- -12-- - -		MATHERS James Sr	21--1- 1--1- - -
JOLLY John	1---1- 3--1- - -		MATHERS Thomas	---1-1 -2--2 - -
JONES Drury	1----1 --1-- - 2		MATHERS William Jr	12--1- 1--1- - -
JONES Jacob	free color 2 2		MATHERS William Sr	-1-211 --1-1 - -
JONES Joana	1----- ---21 - -		MAYNER Stephen	-1---1 3---1 - -
JONES John	11--1- 11-1- - -		MEDLIN Sally	---1-- 21111 - -
JONES Moses	-1---1 -21-- 5 6		MEEKS James	--1-- -1--1 - -
JONES Susannah	----2- ---11 - 1		MEEKS John	3--1-- -1--- - -
JONES William	1---1- 2--1- - -		MEEKS William	1--1-- 1-1-- - -
JONES William	-1--1- 1-11- 3 2		MENACH John	-1--11 2--11 7 3
KEITH John	---1-- 1-1-- - -		METCALFE Thomas	31111- 21-11 3 3
KELLY Thomas	11---1 --1-1 - -		MICHELTREE John	----1- ---1- 1 2
KENNEDY David Sr	-1-211 -22-1 2 1		MILLER James	1---1- 31-1- - -
KENNEDY Robert	2111-1 -2-1- - -		MILLER John	13-1-1 1211- - -
KENTON William	2---1- 2-1-- - 1		MILLER John A	1----1 21-1- - -
KERBY John	3---1- 1-1-- - -		MILLER Stephen	----21 ----1 - 2
KERNS Isam Jr	2--1-- --1-- - 1		MILLER William	2-23-1 112-- - -
KERNS Simeon	-2-1-1 -211- - -		MITCHELL Elijah	1---1- 1-1-1 - -
KERSEY James	---1-- 1-11- - -		MITCHELL Ezekiel	-----1 ---1- - -
KERSEY James Sr	-2-1-1 1-2-1 - -		MITCHELL James	12-1-1 21--1 - -
KERSEY John	---3-1 -22-1 - -		MITCHELL William	1---1- --11- - -
KILLAM Peter	21121- 31-1- - -		MOLER Isaac	22-11- 222-- - -
KIMBROUGH Robert H	2---1- ---1- - -		MOLER Joseph	31--1- 23-11 - -
KIMES George	32111- 2--1- - -		MOLER Lewis	31--1- 2--1- - -
KINCART John	1---1- 1-1-- 2 -		MONSON Samuel	2---1- 111-- 1 -
KNOX David	-----1 -1--1 - -		MONSON Thomas	---1-- --1-- - -
KNOX Samuel	-3--1- --2-- - -		MOORE John	----1- 1-1-- - 1
LAMMS Nancy	------ 11-1- - -		MOORE John	-----1 ----1 - -
LANE Thomas	-2---1 2-2-- - -		MOORE Samuel	1-12-1 -21-1 - -
LAWRENCE William	--11- 2--11 - -		MOORE Thomas	42--1- 22-1- 1 -

Name	Data	Name	Data
MOORE Zedekiah	31--1- 21-1- 2 1	McGILL Alexander	---1-- 2-1-- - -
MORES Saml	1---1- 3-11- - -	McGINNIS Elijah	---1-- --1-- - -
MORGAN Hezekiah	1-11-- --1-- - -	McGINNIS James	3---1- ---1- - -
MORGAN Reese	32-1-1 1121- - -	McGINNIS John	41--1- 1--1- - -
MORGAN Sarah	11-3-- 11--1 - -	McGINNIS Samuel	----1- 2-11- - -
MORRIS Morris	13--1- 2--1- - -	McINNIS Samuel	1--1-- -1--- - -
MORRIS Thomas	32---1 3-11- - -	McINTIRE John	---1-- 1-1-1 - 2
MORRISS Daniel	2---1- 1-1-- - -	McINTIRE Lucy	---1-- --1-1 1 -
MULLIKEN Archibald	21--1- 1--1- 2 1	McMAHAN Robert	2113-1 -21-1 - -
MULLIKEN William	12111- 1--1- - -	McMAHILL John	42--1- 2--1- - -
MURPHY George W	31--1- 31-1- - -	McMAHILL Robert	-1--1- 1-1-1 - 1
MURPHY John	---1-- --1-- 1 -	McMAHILL Thomas	---11- 41-1- 2 -
MUSGROVE Gilbert	-3-111 --2-1 1 -	McMAHILL Wm	1---12 21-1- - -
MUSICK John	22--1- 11-1- - 1	McNEAR James	3---1- --1-- - -
MUSICK Thomas	2---1- ---1- - -	McQUOWN Lawrence	11-2-1 -1--1 - -
MYERS Abraham	1---1- 1-1-- - -	McVEY John	4---1- 1--11 - -
MYERS Christian	1---1- 3--1- - -	McVEY Sarah	--12-- 1---1 - -
MYERS Daniel	----1- ------ - 1	NEAL John	1---1- 2--1- 3 2
MYERS David	21--1- 11-2- - -	NEEVES Danl	1--3-1 -1--1 - -
MYERS George	21--1- 2--1- - -	NELSON Moses	3---1- 11-1- - -
MYERS George	2---1- --1-- - -	NELSON Rachel	-1-1-- -22-1 - -
MYERS Henry	1----1 -1-1- - -	NELSON Thomas	22--1- 3--1- - -
MYERS John	2-131- 2411- - 1	NESBETT William	---1-- 1-1-- - -
MYERS Lewis	3---1- 3--1- - -	NESBITT Sarah	11---- -1111 - -
MYERS Margaret	31-1-- -11-1 - -	NESBITT Thomas	-112-1 -1-21 4 1
MYERS Peter	11--1- 2-1-- - 1	NEWMAN William	1----1 ----1 - -
McANALTY Wm	1--1-- 1-1-- - -	NEWTON John	1---1- 31-1- - -
McANULTY Jane	2----- 1111- - -	NICKASON Mary	-111-- --2-1 - -
McCABE Josiah	--121- 1---2 - 1	NICKLE Robert	-1-1-1 112-1 - -
McCLANAHAN James	--1231 --212 - -	NOAH George	11111- 5211- - -
McCLANAHAN William	32-11- 12-1- - -	NOBLE John	-1-1-1 --2-1 - -
McCLANE Alexander	2--1-- --11- - -	NOE George	11-11- 1--1- 1 3
McCLANE Charles	-----1 --2-1 - -	OLIVA Archibald	-3-11- 41-1- - -
McCLARY Samuel	-111-1 ----1 - -	ORR John	1---1- 4--11 - -
McCLINTOCK Hugh	-1-2-1 --2-1 5 2	OVERBAY Henry	51--1- -1-1- 4 2
McCLINTOCK Joseph	---221 --2-1 1 4	OVERBY Peter	11-11- 4--1- - -
McCLINTOCK Thomas	31--1- 1--1- - -	OWINGS John	11--1- 2--1- - -
McCLINTOCK William	---21- 2-11- - 1	OWINGS Samuel	2--12- 32-12 - 1
McCLINTOCK William	4---1- 1-11- 1 -	PADGET Danl	21---1 1--1- - -
McCONAHAY John	--11-1 -13-1 1 -	PADIN William	----1- 3--1- C 9
McCORMICK James	2--1-- ---1- - -	PARISH Barkley	2---1- -1--- - -
McCORMICK Walter	---21- --111 - -	PARISH David	---1-- 2-1-- - -
McCOY Andrew	1---1- -1-1- - -	PARISH William	----1- 1--1- - -
McCOY Daniel	1--121 --2-- - -	PARKER Charles	2313-1 1-11- - 4
McCOY John	-1-22- --1-1 - -	PARKS James	21--1- 1-1-1 1 -
McCOY John	2--1-1 113-1 3 7	PATTERSON Francis	11--1- 31-1- - -
McCUNE Basil	--1411 111-1 1	PAUGH Solomon	1-12-- --1-- - -
McCUNE Garvin	2---1- 3--1- - -	PAUL Drusilla	1----- 1211- - -
McCUNE John	--1311 111-1 - -	PAULEY Jeremiah	2---1- 2--1- - -
McCUNE Robert	31--11 -2-11 - -	PAULEY John	11--1- 41-1- - -
McCUNE Samuel	----1- --1-- - -	PAULEY William	3---1- 2--1- - -
McDONALD Alexander	---3-1 -11-1 - -	PAULEY Zachariah	1--1-1 1-1-1 - -
McDONALD Eli	3---1- 2--1- - -	PAXTON Daniel	---1-- 1-1-- - -
McDONALD Hugh	2--1-- 2-1-- - -	PAXTON Joseph	----1- ---1- - 1
McDONALD John	21--1- 3--1- - -	PAXTON Robert	3113-1 -111- - -
McDONALD John	1---1- --1-- - -	PAYNE Henry R	21--1- 1111- 4 2
McDONALD Mordecai	-2---1 1-1-1 - -	PEIRCE Mordecai	2---1- 2--1- - -
McDONALD Peter	1----1 2--1- 1 1	PENDERGRASS Edward	1112-1 --1-1 - -
McDONALD Polly	------ 3221- - -	PERRY James	2--11- 2--1- - -
McDONALD Thomas	21--1- 2--1- - -	PEYTON James	---1-- 1-1-- - -
McDOUST Alexander	22--1- 51-1- - -	PEYTON Saml	---1-- --1-- - -
McDOWELL Horatio	--22-- 1-1-- - -	PEYTON Samuel	---2-1 -11-1 - -
McDOWELL James	3---1- 1-1-- - 1	PEYTON Stephen	31-2-1 -21-1 - -
McDOWELL John	3---1- --1-- - -	PEYTON Stephen	21--1- 1--1- - -
McDOWELL Margaret	---2-- --3-1 - -	PEYTON Thomas	-1---1 ----1 - -
McDOWELL William	1----1 ----1 1 2	PEYTON William	1--11- 3--1- - -

PEYTON William	---1--	--1--	-	-	ROBISON George	--11-1	--1-1	-	-
PEYTON William	-----1	2-1--	-	-	ROBISON James	-----1	----1	3	2
PHILIPS Leonard	1----1	--1-1	-	-	ROBISON Jane	-1----	----1	-	-
PIERCY Joseph	----1-	---1-	-	-	ROBISON John	2-111-	41-1-	-	-
PIPER James	12--1-	1-11-	2	5	ROBISON Nathaniel D	-1111-	3-1--	1	3
PIPER Robert	21---1	1-11-	-	-	ROBISON Stephen	-----1	--1-1	-	-
PIPER Saml	1111-1	1-1-1	-	-	ROGERS William	---2--	--1--	-	-
PITT Legram	1--1-	--1--	-	-	ROGERS Willis	---1--	-----	1	1
PLUGH Elias	21-1-1	11-1-	-	-	ROLSTON Robert	2211-1	-11-1	-	-
POE Edmund	1---2	2-2--	-	-	ROSS John	1---1	1-1--	-	-
POE Edmund	1--2--	3-11-	-	-	ROSS Joseph	---1--	1-1--	-	1
POLLOCK James	2----1	22-1-	1	2	ROSS Tilman	1212-1	--1-2	-	-
POTTS George	---1--	2-1--	-	-	RULE Sam	1111-1	2-11-	-	-
POTTS Henry	2---1	1-1--	1		SADLER Edward	11-21-	111-1	2	2
POTTS John	-1--1	5121-	-	-	SAMPLE Polly	--11--	--2-1	-	-
POTTS William	---2-1	1-1-1	-	-	SANDERS James	2--1--	--1--	-	1
POWELL Charles	-1111-	32-1-	-	-	SANDERS James Sr	---1-1	-1--2	-	-
POWELL Isaac	2---1	4--1-	-	-	SANDERSON Mary	-------	1--11	-	-
POWELL Jeremiah	3---1	11111	-	-	SAVETEER William	11--1	1111-	-	1
POWELL John	22--1	11-1-	-	-	SCHWARTZENELDER Peter	-1---1	------	-	-
POWELL Robert	3--1--	--1-1	-	-	SCOTT John	21-11-	21-1-	-	-
POWELL Zenus	-213-1	211-1	-	-	SCOTT Johnathan	22--1	1111-	-	-
PRATHER Barrack	23-1-1	1-211	1	1	SCOTT Josiah	----1	21111	-	-
PRATHER Basil	2---1	1-1--	-	1	SCOTT Nathl	1-121-	3-2--	-	-
PRATHER William	----1-	2-1--	-	-	SCOTT Thomas	-212-1	61-1-	-	-
PUCKETT William	-1--1	1--1-	-	-	SCOTT William	--11--	11---	-	-
PURSLEY Elijah	2---1	3--1-	-	-	SECREST William	11-11-	1-1--	-	-
PURSLEY Jane	-2----	-15-1	-	-	SELBY Barkley	21--1	111--	-	-
PURSLEY Thomas	1---1	1-1--	-	-	SELBY Hasty	1--1--	--1--	-	-
QUETT James	1---1	1--1-	-	-	SELBY Henry	1---1	3-11-	-	-
RAFFE John	1---1	1--1-	-	-	SELBY Isaac	-1--11	21--1	1	-
RANKIN John	1--11-	111--	-	-	SELBY Major	-----1	--1-1	-	1
RANKIN Moses	-2--11	2111-	-	-	SELBY Major	-----1	--1-1	2	4
RAYBURN William	2---1	2-1--	-	-	SELBY William	----1-	--1--	1	1
REAM Adam	1---1	3--1-	3	3	SHANKLIN Benjamin	2---1	2--1-	-	-
REBELIN Martin	---2-1	-11-1	-	-	SHANKLIN John	-1-1-1	1-2-1	-	-
REDDING Roberts	---1--	--1--	-	-	SHANKLIN Sally	-112--	1--1-	-	-
REID James	---1--	1-1--	-	-	SHANNON John	1---1	---1-	-	-
REVEAL Joseph	-1---1	2-1-1	-	-	SHANNON John Jr	---1--	1-1--	-	-
REVEAL Michael	----11	---11	-	-	SHANNON John Sr	3----1	1--1-	-	-
REYNOLDS Dolly	2-----	---1-	-	-	SHANNON Samuel	2--1--	2--1-	-	-
REYNOLDS Richard	21--1	31-1-	-	-	SHARP Isaac	1---1	2--1-	-	-
RHODES Silas	1---1	4---1	-	-	SHARP John T	-111-1	21--1	-	-
RICE Hiram	2--3-1	21-1-	-	-	SHARP Richard	1--1-1	1211-	-	-
RICE William	42-1--	1-21-	-	-	SHAW Lewis	---1--	12-1-	-	-
RICHARDS William	32--1	1111-	-	-	SHAW Margaret	---1--	-12-1	-	1
RICHEY Esau	32--1	-2-1-	-	-	SHEPHERD Joseph	2---1	----1	-	-
RICHEY Henry	2---1	2-11-	-	-	SHICKLES Lord	3---1	2--1-	-	-
RICHEY Isaac	-1---1	11--1	2	4	SHORT Coleman	---1--	2-1--	-	-
RICHEY Isaac Jr	1--1--	---1-	-	-	SHULTZ Abraham	---3--	1-1--	-	-
RICHEY John	4---1	---1-	-	-	SHULTZ Mark	1--1--	--1--	-	-
RICHEY John	---1--	2-1-1	-	-	SHULTZ Peter	2-11-1	3-1-1	-	-
RICHEY Noah	2---1	21-1-	-	-	SHUMATE Bailey	1--1-1	----1	-	-
RICHEY Solomon	42--1	2-11-	4	1	SHUMATE Peyton	-1-54-	42-1-	1	3
RICHEY Zachariah	1--1--	2-1--	-	-	SIMMS Joseph	----1	4-1--	2	1
RIGGIN Jesse	-----1	--1-1	-	-	SLAUGHTER Bartholomew	-----1	--1--	3	3
RIGGS Erasmus	2--1-1	134-1	-	-	SLEDD Sarah	21-1--	-111-	-	1
RILEY John	---1-1	2221-	1	1	SLOOP James	2--1--	1-1--	-	-
RILEY Saml	1---1	111--	-	-	SLOOP Margaret	11-1--	--1-1	-	-
ROBERTS Alexander	22---1	3--11	-	-	SMART Humphrey	3---1	2--1-	-	-
ROBERTS Henley	1313-2	21-1-	-	-	SMART Saml	----1	---1-	-	-
ROBERTS James	1---1	2-1--	-	-	SMART William	3--1--	--1--	-	-
ROBERTS Thomas	-211-1	51-1-	-	-	SMART john	2---2	1-1--	-	-
ROBERTSON Samuel	1-1211	-11-1	-	-	SMEDLEY Aran Jr	1--11-	--1--	-	-
ROBINS Spencer	----1-	2--1-	-	-	SMEDLEY Aron Sr	-1-1-1	--1--	1	1
ROBINSON James	1--11-	2--1-	-	-	SMILEY Robert	----2-	211--	-	-

Name	Census
SMITH Hezekiah	4211-1 -121- - -
SMITH James	--13-1 211-1 - -
SMITH James	2211-1 -1--1 - -
SMITH John	----1- ---1- 3 -
SMITH Mitchell	2----1 2---1 - -
SMITH Nathan	11-1-- --1-- - -
SMITH Philip	---2-- 1-1-- 1 -
SMITH Thomas	1---1- 1-1-- - -
SMITH William	4111-1 1121- - 2
SMITH William	---1-1 1-1-1 - -
SNAP Daniel	1---1- 3--1- - -
SNAP George	41-1-- -211- - -
SNAP George Jr	3---1- ---1- 1 -
SNAP Peter	--13-1 1---1 - -
SNAP Samuel	----1- ---1- - -
SPARKS Caleb	22--1- 3--1- - -
SPARKS Catherine	---11- 112-1 - -
SPARKS Catherine	-1---- 3-2-1 - -
SPARKS George	22---1 1-11- - -
SPHAR Jacob	12--1- 11-1- - -
SPHARS Henry	1----1 22111 - -
SQUIRES Margaret	2212-- 11--1 - 1
STANDIFORD James	1---2- 2-11- - -
STARK John	--22-1 -31-1 - -
STARK Thomas	2--11- --1-- - -
STEARS John	2---1- -1--1 - -
STEELE Jesse	31---- 134-1 - -
STEEPLEY Benjamin	---1-- 1-1-- - -
STEPHENSON Elizabeth	---1-- 112-1 - -
STEPHENSON George	-----1 ----1 - -
STEPHENSON John	---1-- 1--1- - -
STEPHENSON Joseph	41--1- -1-1- - -
STEPHENSON Rebeckah	1----- --111 - -
STEPHENSON Robert	2---1- 3--1- - -
STEPHENSON Roberts	52--1- -1-1- - -
STEPHENSON Thomas	-1-1-- 1-1-- - -
STEPHENSON William	1---1- 1-1-- - -
STEPHENSON William	1--1-- --1-- - -
STEWART Abel	-----1 ---1- - -
STEWART Thomas	---1-- --1-- - -
STEWART Willoby	4-11-1 2-21- - -
STITES Richard	-211-1 --1-1 - -
STITT James	1--1-- --1-- - -
STITTS Hugh	-1---1 -1--1 2 5
STOKES Benjamin	---11- 4-2-1 - -
STOKES Thomas	----1- ---1- - -
STONE Joshua	-2-1-1 1---1 5 5
STOOPS James	1---1- 2--1- - -
STOOPS John	32--1- 1--1- - -
STOOPS Moses	3---1- 4--1- - -
STOOPS Philip	21-2-1 31-12 - -
STOOPS William	23---1 42-1- - -
STOOPS William	----1- 3-1-- - -
STOUT William	3122-1 11-1- - -
STURMAN Valentine	11-1-1 1-1-1 - -
SUDDETH Francis	11--1- 4211- - 1
SUMMETT George	---1-- --2-1 - -
SUMMETT Jacob	----1- --1-- - -
SUMMETT James	----1- 1-1-- 1 -
SUTTERS Uriah	3---1- 1-1-- - -
SWART George	12-1-- -11-1 - -
SWEARINGEN Hezekiah	-1--1- --11- - -
SWEARINGEN Josiah	1---1- -1-1- - -
SWENEY Thomas	----1- 4--1- - -
TARR Charles	1----1 21-1- 3 4
TAYLOR George	12---1 31-1- - -
TAYLOR John	-2---1 ----1 - -
TAYLOR John	----1- 2---1 - -
TAYLOR John Jr	---1-- 1-1-- - -
TENNEY John	-1---1 -21-1 - -
TERRY Reuben	1211-1 1---1 - -
THOMAS Edward	2111-1 3121- - -
THOMAS Howard	3212-1 11-1- 2 5
THOMAS John	1--1-- 1--11 - -
THOMAS Rosie	4112-1 2-11- - -
THOMASON Landy	2----1 31-1- - -
THOMPSON Daniel	11--1- 3--1- - -
THOMPSON Henry	1---11 --111 - -
THOMPSON James H	33111- 1-121 - -
THOMPSON John	2--1-1 231-1 - -
THOMPSON Sarah	1----- 11-11 - -
THOMPSON Susan	--12-- ---1- - -
THOMSON James	4---1- 11-1- - 1
THOMSON Saml	1---1- 1-1-- - -
THOMSON William	---111 -11-1 - -
THROCKMORTON John	21--1- 21-1- 4 3
THROCKMORTON Thomas	3----1 232-1 4 3
THROCKMORTON Thomas Sr	------1 ----- 5 5
TOWLER Luke	21--1- 11-1- 4 4
TOWNSEND Joseph M	1--1-- --1-- - -
TOWNSEND Joshua	1--2-1 411-1 - -
TOWNSEND Peter	---1-- 1-1-- 5 1
TOWNSEND William	1---1- 2--1- - -
TOWNSEND William	--11-1 32--1 - -
TRIGG Thomas	11-1-1 -2-11 1 1
TRUETT Thomas	1--1-- -11-- 2 2
TUCKER Samuel	22--1- 3111- - -
TULL Hardy	1----1 12--1 1 2
TULL Jesse	31-111 21-1- - -
TULL John	32--1- 2-11- - -
TURLEY Charles B	2112-- -1-1- - 1
TURNER Robert	---1-- 4-1-- - -
TUTTLE Peter	2---11 4--11 - -
ULRICK Saml	---21- ----- 4 3
UTTERBACK Benjamin	-----1 1--1- - -
UTTERBACK Harman	---1-1 -1-21 - -
UTTERBACK John	---11- ---1- 2 1
UTTERBACK Washington	2--1-- 1-1-- - -
VANSKOEKE Josiah	23--1- 3-11- - -
VAUGHAN James	11-1-- 1-2-1 2 -
VICTOR James	------1 1-111 2 4
VICTOR John	1--11- 1-1-- - -
VICTOR William	42--1- 1--1- - -
WADDLE John	2---1- 2--1- - -
WADDLE Joseph	21--1- 1211- - -
WAGGONER Richard	2--1-- --1-- - -
WALLACE John	---1-- 1--1- - -
WALLACE Sarah	-1-2-- ----1 - -
WALLER Valentine	-1---1 21-1- - -
WARD Andrew	11---1 -1211 - -
WARD John R	3---1- ---1- 3 3
WARD William	---1-- 2-1-- - -
WARDLOW Joseph	----1- ---1- - -
WAUGH Samuel M	12-1-1 111-1 - -
WEATHERFORD Jonas	3---1- --1-- 1 -
WEBB Charles	21---1 21-1- - -
WEBSTER Isaac	31--1- 31-1- - -
WELLS Nathan	2-111- 3--1- - -
WELLS Ruth	3112-- -21-1 - -
WEST Adam	1---1- 1-1-- - -
WEST Amos	2-11-1 12311 - -
WEST Carey	2611-- 1-11- - -

Name	Col 1	Col 2			Name	Col 1	Col 2		
WEST Elijah	2---1-	1-11-	-	-	WILLS James	43---1	21-1-	-	-
WEST Isaac	---1-1	--1-1	-	-	WILLS Robert	1--1--	--1--	-	-
WEST Jane	11----	1-11-	-	-	WILLS John	12-3-1	-11-1	-	-
WEST John	1---1-	3-1--	-	-	WILSON Uriah	3---11	1-1-1	-	-
WEST Philip	-1--1-	4--1-	-	-	WILSON Benjamin	-----1	1--11	-	-
WEST Thomas	-113-1	-211-	-	-	WILSON Benjamin	3---1-	22-1-	-	-
WHALEY John	-3-11-	--21-	-	-	WILSON Catherine	------	--2-1	1	1
WHEATLEY Thomas	----21	--1--	-	-	WILSON Charles	23---1	1--1-	-	-
WHEELER Joseph	33121-	1--1-	-	-	WILSON David	2---1-	2-1--	-	-
WHEELER William	2112-1	3--1-	-	-	WILSON Jeremiah	1--1--	--1--	1	-
WHISTLER Mary	1-----	1--1-	-	-	WILSON Jesse	1---1-	---1-	-	-
WHITE Ebenezer	1--1--	--1--	-	-	WILSON John	2---1-	1--11	-	-
WHITE John	-2--21	--2--	-	-	WILSON John	-1---1	-34-1	-	-
WHITE Stephen	1--1--	--1--	-	-	WILSON Stephen	3---1-	---1-	-	-
WHORTON Eli	1----1	1---1	-	-	WISHARD Samuel	22---1	21-1-	1	-
WHORTON Joseph	11-11-	2211-	-	-	WOOD George	2----1	1-1--	-	-
WIGGINS John	2-11-1	1--11	-	-	WOOD John	21111-	31-1-	-	-
WIGGINS William	1---1-	3--1-	-	-	WOOD John	-1---1	111--	-	2
WILCOXON Josiah	11-11-	---1-	-	-	WOOD Joseph	-1-1-	4--1-	-	-
WILEY Hugh	21-11-	33-11	-	-	WOOD Nimrod	---1--	1-1--	1	2
WILEY Robert	21-11-	11-1-	-	-	WOOD William	3---1-	1--1-	-	-
WILLIAMS Abraham	2---1-	1--1-	-	-	WORKMAN John	3---1-	2-1--	-	-
WILLIAMS Benjamin	1----1	-1--1	-	-	WORKMAN Samuel	1---1-	3--1-	-	-
WILLIAMS John	-2-1-1	1-2-1	-	-	WRIGHT Edward	2-1--	--1--	-	-
WILLIAMS John	-2-1-1	1-2-1	-	-	WYCOFF Ephraim	2---1	12-1-	-	-
WILLIAMS Nathan	1---1-	2-1--	-	5	YATES Alesey	-2----	---1-	-	-
WILLIAMS Samuel	---1--	------	-	-	YOUNG Jacob	11-1-1	-24-1	-	1
WILLIAMS William J	1---1-	3-1-1	-	-	YOUNGER Joshua	-1-1-1	1-1-1	-	-
WILLS David	3----1	-311-	-	-	ZILER Jacob	3--11-	--1--	-	-

Name	Census		Name	Census
ADAIR Benjamin	-1211--1------ --11--1------ - -		ASBERRY Mary	---1---------- -------1------ - -
ADAIR Richard	-311--1------ 2-11-1------- - -		ASHBROOK Andrew	21-1-1------- 11---1------- - -
ADAIR William	------1------ --11-1------- 9 -		ASHCRAFT Ephraim	--------1---- ----2--1----- - -
ADAMS Aron	-----1------ ----1------- - -		ASHCRAFT Nimrod	1-2-1-------- 111-1-------- - -
ADAMS Ephraim	2-21--1------ -111-1-1----- - -		ASHCRAFT William	1---1-------- 21--1------- - -
ADAMS Joseph	12----1------ 111--1------- - -		ASHLEY James P	-11----1----- 1---1------- - -
ADAMS Thomas	1---1------- ----1-2------ - -		ATKINSON William	2-----1------ 13---1------- - -
ADAMS Thomas Sr	--11---1----- ----1------- - -		BAILY Elisha	----1-------- ---1-------- - -
ADAMS William	------1------ 1---1------- - -		BAIRD James	------1------ ------1------ - -
AINSWORTH Charles	-1-----1------ -2---1------- - -		BAKER Fullerton	1-112--1----- -111---1----- 1 -
ALEXANDER Harvey	1---2-------- ----1------- - -		BAKER John	22-1--1------ --1---1------ D -
ALEXANDER James	2-----1------ 1---1------- - -		BAKER Peter	----1-------- --1--------- - -
ALEXANDER James	1---1------- ----1------- - -		BAKER William	----1-------- ----1------- 2 -
ALEXANDER Jesse	11-11-1------ 1--1------- - -		BAKER mary	------------- ----------1-- 3 -
ALEXANDER John	-21--1------- 31---1------- - -		BANISTER John	---------1--- ----1-------- - -
ALEXANDER Thomas	122--1------- 1--111--1----- - -		BANISTER John Jr	1-1--1------- 211--1------- - -
ALLEN Douglas	22---1------- 11---1------- - -		BANISTER Thomas	12---1------- 21---1------- - -
ALLEN James	2-----1------ ------1------ - -		BARKSHIRE William G	---11-------- ----1------- - -
ALLEN Jesse	322--1------- -1--1------- - -		BARLOW John	322---1------ 1-----2------ - -
ALLEN John	1111--1------ 2211-1------- - -		BARLOW John	--111--1----- -112--1------ 2 -
ALLEN Joseph	---1----1----- -2221-1------ - -		BARLOW Thomas	-----1------- 11----1------ - -
ALLISON Alfred	1---1------- 1---1------- - -		BARLOW William	----2---1---- --------1----- 6 -
ALLISON Betty	--12-------- ------1------ - -		BARNETT Ambros	2--11---1---- -1--1--1----- - -
ANDERSON Daniel	-11-1------- 3111-1------- - -		BARNETT John	12---1------- ----1-------- - -
ANDERSON James	1---1------- ----1--1----- - -		BARNETT John Jr	---212-1----- 1-11--1------ - -
ANDERSON John	-11-1---1---- --------1---- - -		BARNETT Moses	-11----1---- 11111-1------ - -
ARCHER Sampson	12-11--1----- ---12-1------ - -		BARNETT Robert	1---11------ 1-111-------- - -
ARDRY Robert	-1----1------- -------1-1---- - -		BARNETT William	11---1------ 122--1------- - -
ARMSTRONG James	------1------ 1---1------- - -		BARR Robert	12-3--1------ 111--1------- - -
ARNETT Samuel	---21--1----- -------1----- D -		BARTLETT Samuel	--221--1------ ---11-1------- - -
ARNOLD James	11---1------- 21--1------- - -		BASKET Jesse Sr	11--1---1---- 222----1----- 5 -
ARNOLD Lewis G	-1--1--1---- --11-11------ A -		BASKETT John	22---1------- 1---1------- 3 -
ARNOLD Matthew R	-----2-------- -11-11------- 4 -		BASKETTS Robt	1---1-------- 1---1------- - -

NICHOLAS COUNTY KENTUCKY 1830 CENSUS

BATSON John	-12---1-------	BLACKBURN Benjamin	-1--1--------
	2--2-1-------- - -		11--1-------- - -
BATY James	----1---------	BLACKBURN Joseph	-1--1--------
	11--1-------- - -		--1--1-------- - -
BAXTER George	----1---------	BLACKBURN Samuel	----1----1---
	----32------- - -		--------1---- - -
BAXTER William	1--1---------	BLACKMAN Samuel	----1----1---
	1---1-------- 1 -		--------1---- - -
BEANDON Joseph	---13---1-----	BLACKMORE Tho W	1---1--------
	------------ - -		2---1-------- 2
BEARD Jacob	1---1---------	BLAIR Alexander	---1----1----
	----1-------- - -		--1------1--- 2 -
BEARD Wm	21---1--------	BLAIR Alexander Jr	-11-11--------
	11---1-------- - -		----2-------- 1 -
BEATY David	----1--------	BLAIR James B	------1--------
	----1-------- - -		----11-------- 3 -
BECKNER Abram	-1---1--------	BLOUNT Elizabeth	--------------
	2---1-------- - -		---111-1----- - -
BECKNER Jacob L	1-----1-------	BLOUNT Hezekiah	1-11-1--------
	11--1---1----- 2 -		111--1-------- - -
BECKNER Peter	1---2---------	BLOUNT Wm	21--1--------
	----1-------- - -		11---1-------- - -
BEDINGER Geo M Jr	1---21--------	BOARDMAN James	21---1------
	----1-------- 3 -		-1---1-------- - -
BEDINGER George	-1--1-----1---	BOATMAN George	----1--------
	--1-11-1------ D -		1---1-------- 1 1
BELL Losson	2-------------	BOATMAN Robert	1---1--------
	-12--1-------- - -		2---1---1---- - -
BELL Robert	-2---1--------	BOATMAN Robert	1---11-------
	1--1-1-------- - -		22--11--------
BELL William	3-----1-------	BOATMAN William	-------1------
	------------ - -		--2---1-------- - -
BELL William	1---1---1----	BORDMAN Benjamin	1---1--1-----
	1---21--1---- - -		11--1--1--1-- - -
BELLOS Jacob	311--1--------	BOSLEY Elijah	----1--------
	1-1-1-------- 1 -		2---1-------- - -
BELLOWS Philip	31---1--------	BOSLEY Elizabeth	----2--------
	1-11-1-------- - -		---2---1----- - -
BENIGAL Neal	1-1-1---------	BOSLEY James	1----1-------
	----1-------- 4 -		2---1-------- 1 -
BENINGALL David	----1---1----	BOSLEY William	1---1-1-------
	-11121--1---- 2 -		1---1-------- 1 -
BENZ Jesse	22-1-1--------	BOWEN William	--11-----1---
	1---1-------- 1 -		-1--------1--- - -
BERRY Francis	1-1--1--------	BOWENS John	-1--1--------
	1111-1-------- - -		2---1-------- - -
BERRY Geo	112------1----	BOWIN Francis	113----1-----
	-111--1-------- - -		2111--1-------- - -
BERRY Robert	---12---1----	BOWIN James	1---1--------
	-11--1-------- 8 -		1---1-------- - -
BIRAM Augustine	11112-1-------	BOWLS Mary	----3--------
	1-22-1-------- 2 -		-----11--1--- - -
BIRCHFIELD Elias	--1---1-------	BOYD John	--12-2--------
	--12-1-------- - -		--1-1-------- - -
BISHOP Charles	11---1--------	BOYD Samuel	-2---1-------
	21--1-------- - -		-------------- - -
BISHOP Daniel	-11--1--------	BOYD Thomas	--1--1--------
	--1--1-------- 1 -		-------------- 2 -
BISHOP Henry	2---2---------	BRADLEY Geo	--112--1-----
	1---2-------- - -		-1-1---1-----
BISHOP Henry	1311---1------	BRADLEY Geo Jr	------1-------
	12----1-------- - -		-----1-------- - -
BISHOP Richard	-1--21--------	BRADSHAW Alexander	1---1----1---
	1-12-1---1--- - -		2---1-------- - -
BLACK Alexander	1---1---------	BRADSHAW Polly	2-------------
	--1---------- - -		-211-11------- - -

Name	Census tally (line 1 / line 2)
BRADY Patrick	-11-1---------- / -1113-1------- - -
BRADY William	------1-------- / ------1-------- - -
BRANCH Edward	------1-------- / 22--1--------- - -
BRANCH Pleasant	----1-----1-- / --2-----1---- 8 3
BRANS John	--1-11-1----- / ------11----- - -
BRECKENRIDGE Mary	---1--------- / ---------1--- - -
BRECKENRIDGE Preston	2---1-------- / ----1-------- - -
BRECKENRIDGE Wash´ton	----1-------- / ---1--------- - -
BRENTON John	1---1-------- / 1--1-------- - -
BRENTON Samuel	--11--1------ / ---------1--- - -
BRIAN Daniel	12---1------- / 2-1--1------- 5 -
BRIAN Geo	1---1----1--- / 1211---------- D -
BRIERLY George	-----------1-- / -1--------1--- - -
BRIERLY George	-----------1-- / 11------1---- - -
BRIERLY Thomas	-1---1-------- / --1-11-------- - -
BRIERLY Thomas	-----1-------- / -----1-------- - -
BROOKIN Vivian	-11--1-------- / -2-1--1---1-- 9 -
BROOKS Mosely R	1---1-------- / ----1-------- - -
BROOKS Zachariah	--111--1------ / --2-----1----- 8 -
BROTHERTON Edward B	1--22-------- / ----1-------- 1 -
BROWN Ann	----2-------- / ---------1--- - -
BROWN Archibald	-11------1---- / --12-1-1----- 1 -
BROWN Cletus	-------1------ / -----1-------- - -
BROWN Daniel	22---1-------- / 1-2-1--------- - -
BROWN John Sr	----1-----1--- / ---11----1--- 5 -
BROWN Lanvil	-1--1-------- / -1--1--------- - -
BROWN Milton	-1---1-------- / 211-1--------- - -
BROWN Samuel L	---12-------- / ----1--1----- - -
BUCHANAN James	211--1-------- / -21---1------- 5 -
BUCKLER Stephen	----1--1----- / ---12----1--- - -
BUCKLER Stephen	2-1--1-------- / --1--2-------- - -
BUCKLER Wilson	-1----1------- / 2---1--------- - -
BUCKNER Samuel	-------1------ / -------------- 2 6
BUNTON James	--1-1--1---- / --12-1------- - -
BUNTON John	----2-------- / 1-1--------- - -
BUNTON William	--213---1---- / 12-1--1------ - -
BURDEN Charles	---------1--- / -21-1--1----- - -
BURDEN Elijah	1---1-------- / 1-1-1-------- - -
BURDEN James	1-1--1------- / -3-11-------- - -
BURDEN Janat	1---1-------- / ---1--------- - -
BURDEN Sally	-------------- / -1--1-------- - -
BURDEN Samuel	112--1------- / 11-1-1------- - -
BURNES Andrew	21---1------- / ----1-------- - -
BURNES John	2122--1------ / ---1-1------- - -
BURNS James	--2-1-1------ / -1-1-1------- 1 -
BURNS Matthew	-11---1------ / --11--1------ - -
BURNS Robert	----11------ / ----1-------- - -
BURNS Robert	1---1-------- / 221--1------- - -
BURNS Samuel	111--1------- / 22--1-------- - -
BURNS William	------1------ / --1-1---1---- - -
BURNS William	-1-1---1----- / ---11-------- - -
BUSBY Archibald	-------1------ / 11--1-------- - -
BUSBY Charles	11---1------- / 121-----1--- - -
BUTLER Joseph D	121111------- / 21--1-------- - -
BYERS John	---1--1------ / --21--1------ - -
CALDWELL Alexander	-11---1------ / -221-1------- - -
CALDWELL Alexander Jr	1---1-------- / ----1--------- - -
CALDWELL Anna	2--1--------- / -12--1-------- - -
CALDWELL David A	----1-------- / 1---1-1------- - -
CALDWELL David B	13-1---1----- / 1-1--1-------- - -
CALDWELL David C	1-1--1------- / --1------1--- - -
CALDWELL David R	13-1---1----- / 11--1---------
CALDWELL James	11---1------- / 2----1-------
CALDWELL James	-12--1------- / 21---1-------
CALDWELL James	121--1------- / ---11--1-----
CALDWELL James M	1111--1------- 5 - / 1---1--------- - -

CALDWELL John	312---1------ -21--1------ - -	CASSIDAY David	----1-------- 1---1-------- - -
CALDWELL Margaret	1------------ -22--1------ - -	CASSIDAY James Jr	1-11--1------ ---1--1------ - -
CALDWELL Robert	----------1--- ----1---1---- - -	CASSIDAY Nelly	------------- --1--11------ - -
CALDWELL Robt	---21--1---- -12--1------ - -	CASSIDAY William	11--1---1---- ---1--1------ - -
CALDWELL Thomas	1-111--1---- -1-12-------- - -	CASSIDY James Jr	1---1-------- 1---1-------- - -
CALDWELL Thomas	-1--1-------- -----1------ - -	CASSIDY Jeremiah	1---11------- ----1-------- - -
CALDWELL William	-2------1---- -2------1---- - -	CAUGHY James	-11--1------- 22---1------- - -
CALDWELL William Jr	-----1------- -111-1------- K -	CHADWICK Isaac	------1------ --------1---- - -
CALL William	-111-1------- 112---1------ - -	CHADWICK John	-1--1-------- ----1-------- - -
CALLAWAY John	-1211--1----- 1-11--1------- - -	CHANEY John	---2---1----- -------1------ 4 -
CALVERT Jesse	---------1---- ---11---1---- - -	CHANEY William	----1---1---- -------1----- 5 -
CALVERT Page	--21-1-------- -3---1------- - -	CHANEY William Jr	1---1--1----- 11--1--------- - -
CALVERT William	121--1-------- 21--1--------- - -	CHAPPELL Edward	11---1------- ----1-------- 1 -
CAMPBELL Francis	-2-11--1----- ---1--1------ - -	CHERIS Thomas M	----1-------- --1---------- - -
CAMPBELL Geo	211--1------- -1----1------ - -	CHIPLEY John	------1------ 11111-------- - -
CAMPBELL Hugh	13-----1------ -1---1-------- 1 -	CIDLE Thomas	2---1-------- 11--1--------- - -
CAMPBELL James	1---1--------- 1----1---1--- - -	CLARK Alexander	1---1-------- 21--1--1----- - -
CAMPBELL James	121-2-1------- 11-3---------- - -	CLARK James	2----1------- --1-1--------- - -
CAMPBELL John	----1-------- ---1--------- - -	CLARK Jeremiah	-1121-1------ ----1-1------ 6 -
CAMPBELL John	1--21--1----- 132---1------ - -	CLARK Joseph	---31-------- 2---1--------- - -
CAMPBELL Joseph	--2--1-------- 21--1--------- - -	CLARK Nancy	--1--1------- --------2---- 9 -
CAMPBELL Joseph Sr	1--11-------- -2-11--------- - -	CLARK Samuel	--111--1----- -11----1----- - -
CAMPBELL Josiah	--1----1------ -----1-1----- - -	CLARK Thomas	2----1------- 1---1-------- 1 -
CAMPBELL Robt	111---1------- -11--1-------- - -	CLARK Wadda	1------------ 1---1-------- - -
CAMPBELL Robt	11-2----1---- 1-2---1------- 5 -	CLAUGHTON Elisha	-1---1------- 2---1-------- 1 -
CAMPBELL William	1-11-1-------- 22--1---1---- - -	CLAY James	-----1---1--- ----1------- 6 -
CAMPBELL Williamson	21---1------- 12---1------- - -	CLAY John	----1-------- ---1-------- 1 -
CAMRON John	11----1------- 11---1-------- - -	CLAYPOOLE John	---1--------- ---1--------- - -
CAR George	11---1------- 212--1------- 1 -	CLAYPOOLE Washington	2---1-------- ----1-------- - -
CARRINGTON William	1---1-------- 11--1-------- - -	CLAYTON Lemuel	------------- -------1----- - 3
CARTER Crawford	-1------1----- 2111--1------ - -	CLAYTON William	11----1------ 111-1-------- - -
CARTER John	11-2-1-------- 111--1------- 4 -	COLIVER Andrew	----1----1--- ---1--------- - -
CARTER Thomas	----1--------- 2---1--------- - -	COLLIER Coleman A	----1-1------ ---1-1------- 5 -

COLLIER Hamlet	--111--1------ --1-2--1------ 8 -	CRAIG Geo	----1--------- 1---1--------- - -
COLLIER James H	-----1-------- ----1--------- 5 -	CRAIG George	----1--------- 1---1--------- - -
COLLIER John	1-1-1--------- 1---1--------- 7 -	CRAIG John	----1--------- 1---1--------- - -
COLLIER Joseph	-----1-------- 2--1--------- 4 -	CRAIG Robert	----1--------- 21--1--------- - -
COLLIER William	---1----1----- --21---1------ K -	CRAWFORD Alexander B	-21--1-------- 211---1-------
COLLIER Wm	1---1--------- 2---1--------- 4 -	CRAWFORD Thornton	1---1--------- 1---1--------- - -
COLLIERS John W	1---1--------- 1---1--------- - -	CRAWFORD William	-1-21-1------- 1-1--2---1---- - -
COLLINS Edward	-21-1--1------ 1-2--1-------- 6 -	CRAY Martin	--13--1------- 1---1--------- 1 -
COLLINS Elijah	---1---1------ ---2---1------ - -	CRAYCRAFT Thomas	----1--------- 31--1--------- - -
COLLINS Thomas	-11----1------ 11-11-1------- - -	CRESS Elizabeth	---12--------- --------1----- 6 -
CONIERS Azariah	-111-1-------- --11--1------- - -	CROSE Jonathan	1213-1-------- ----1--------- - -
CONIERS Enoch	1---1--------- 31--1--------- 1 -	CROSS Benjamin	1-1--1-------- --1-1--------- - -
CONN James	1-3--1-------- 211-1--------- G -	CROUCH Abraham	1---1--------- 1---1--------- 2 -
CONWAY John Jr	1----1---1---- 1---1---1----- 5 -	CROUCH Ambrose D	21---1-------- 1----1-------- - -
CONWAY John Jr	11---1-------- 11--1--------- 4 1	CROUCH David	----1---1----- -1-1-1--1----- 4 -
CONWAY Wiliam	211-11-------- --1--1-------- 4 -	CROUCH John	----11--1----- -1-1--1-------
COOK Martin B	--1--1-------- 111-1--------- - -	CROUCH Jonathan	11211-1------- 121-1--------- 4 -
COOK Peter	---2--1------- ----1--------- - -	CRUMP Beverly	1---1--------- 1------------- - -
COOK William	-----1---1---- --------1----- 5 -	CRUMP Elisha	13----1------- 123---1-1---- - -
COONS Elijah	2----1-------- ----1--------- 1 -	CRUMP Joseph	1----1-------- 1----1-------- - -
COONS Joseph	1---1--------- 1---1--------- 1 -	CUMBERS Thomas	1----1-------- 1---1-------- - -
COONS Thomas	-----1-------- 1------------- - -	CUNNINGHAM Robert	1----2-------- 12--11---1--- - -
COPER Bates	22--1--------- 1--11--------- - -	CUNNINGHAM Wm	2---1--------- ----1-------- - -
CORBIN Joshua	1----1-------- ---11--1------ 3 -	CURTIS Job	-----1-------- 1----1-------- 1 -
CORRELL Hugh	1---1--------- 1---1--------- - -	CURTIS Seth	--------1----- ---------1---- - -
CORRELL Lewis	--1----1------ -1-2---1------ 2 -	DALE Isaac	3-1---1------- -11--1-------- 7 -
COTINGHAM Barkley	----1--------- ----1--------- - -	DALE John	---11--------- ------------- 1 -
COTINGHAM John	2---1--------- ----1--------- - -	DALE Pernal	----1--------- 1--1---------- - -
COTINGHAM William	-112-1--1----- 3211-1-------- 1 -	DALLAS William	1--1---------- ------1-------
COUCHMAN Andrew	---22--------- ----1--1------ 1 -	DALZELL John	----1-1------- 2----1--------
COUCHMAN Michael	1---1--------- 1--11--------- 1 -	DALZELL Katherine	-2--1--1------ 1-1----------- - -
COUGH Alexander	1----1-------- ----1--------- - -	DALZELL Thomas	-1-1-1-------- - - 11--1-----1---
COWIN Hugh	--111--1------ --121-1------- - -	DAMPIER Henry	---1---1------ - - -1-1--1------- 1131--1------- - -

DARRELL George	-------1------ -------1---- 8 -	DOTSON Dudley	--1---1------ -1-1--1------ - -
DARRELL Henry D	----1--------- --1-------- 3 -	DOTSON Elijah	2-2---1------ 1-12-1------- - -
DAVIDSON James	1----1-------- -11-1------- - -	DOTSON John	2--------1--- ----1------- - -
DAVIDSON John	12---1-------- 1-1--1------ - -	DOUGHERTY	-----1------- -1--1------ 4 -
DAVIDSON John	-1---1-------- 21---2------ 1 -	DOUGHERTY Isaac	---11-------- ---12-------- - -
DAVIDSON Thomas	--------1---- --------1---- 2 -	DOUGHERTY John	-1--11---1--- --11---1---- - -
DAVIS Joshua	11----1------- 21--1------ - -	DOWNIE James	1---1-------- ---1-------- - -
DAYTON Jonathan	----1--------- ---1-------- - -	DOWNIE John	2----1------- -1--1------- - -
DAZEY Elijah	-------1------ -------1------ 7 -	DOWNIE Sarah	---1-------- --11-1------ - -
DAZEY Ishmael	-11-1-1------ 1211-1------- - -	DRYDEN Martha	---1--------- --11--1----- - -
DAZEY Lemuel	---11--1----- -------1---- 3 -	DUDLEY James	2----1------- 1---1------ 1 -
DEAN Abraham	21--1--------- ----1------- - -	DURROUGH Sarah	--11--------- -111-1----- - -
DEAN Alexander	1---1--------- -2--1------- - -	DURROUGH William	----2-------- ----------- - -
DEAN John B	1111--1------ -111--1----- - -	DUTY John	---1-------- -1--1------- 1 -
DEATLA Jemima	--121-------- 1--1---1---- - -	DYER William	------------ --------1--- - -
DELAY Polly	--1---------- 1122--1----- - -	DYKES Robert	------1------ 1-31--1------ 6 -
DERICKSON Job	------------- ------------ - A	EADES Thomas	--12----1--- -1-1---1---- - -
DEVINS Gilead	111---------- 2----1----- - -	EALES Geo	2121-1------- -1---1---1--- 1 -
DEVONS William	1----1------- 1----1----- 5 -	EARLYWINE Daniel	11--1-------- 11-11------- - -
DEWIT Jacob	111---1------ 1122-1------ - -	EARLYWINE David	21-1-1------- --2--1------ - -
DICKERSON Daniel	----1-------- 1---1------ - -	EARLYWINE Mary	------------ --------1--- - -
DICKERSON Isaac	11--1-------- ----1---1--- - -	EARLYWINE William	11---1------- 12---1------ - -
DINSMORE David	-2--1--------- 1--11------ - -	EATON Elijah	2---1-------- ----1------- - -
DINSMORE Henry	1-1---1------- -11---1----- 1 -	EATON Jacob	---1---1----- ---1-1-1---- - -
DINSMORE James	23--1--------- ------1----- - -	EATON Shaffie	-----1------- 1---1------- - -
DINSMORE Katherine	1---1--------- ---11-1-1--- - -	EDWARD John	-1--1--1----- -2121-1------ - -
DINSMORE Samuel	-1---1--1----- 2---1------ - -	EDWARDS Benjamin	--1-1--1----- ---21------ - -
DOLEN James	----1--------- 1---1------- 1 -	EDWARDS Robert	1----1------- 311-1---1---- 4 -
DOLEN John	---1-11------ ---1---1---- - 1	ELLIOTT Anna	23-2--------- -121--1------ - -
DORRAH Samuel	----2--------- ----------- - -	ELLIOTT Robert	--1-3---1---- -1-2-1------ - -
DOTIS Skillman	--1--1-------- 311--1----- - -	ELLIS Mary	-----1------- --------1---- 2 -
DOTIS Thomas	----------1-- --------1---- - -	ENDICOT Joseph	-------1------ --222--1----- - -
DOTIS William	--1----1----- ------1----- - -	ENDICOT Samuel	1---1-------- ----1------- - -

ERNEST John `2-1--1---------` / `-31--1-------- - -`
ERVIN Franklin `2---1---------` / `1----1-------- - -`
ERVIN Lloyd `-21---1-------` / `2-23---------- - -`
EUBANKS Joseph Jr `----1---------` / `---1---------- - -`
EUBANKS Joseph L `----2--1-----` / `--111--------- 7 -`
EUBANKS Wm `111--1--------` / `12---1-------- 1 -`
EVANS David `2--11---------` / `12---1-------- - -`
EVANS Joseph `----1---------` / `2---1--------- - -`
EVANS Ludwig `111---1-------` / `1-11-1-------- G -`
FARRAND Chapman `1---1---------` / `----1--------- - -`
FEEBACK Gilbert `231--1--------` / `1----1-------- - -`
FEEBACK Jacob `21-1-1--------` / `-111-1-------- - -`
FEEBACK John `22-1--1-------` / `--21-1-------- - -`
FEEBACK Mary `--12----------` / `11---1---1---- - -`
FIELD Abraham `121---1-------` / `-3----1------- - -`
FIELDER George `---------1----` / `---2----1---- 9 -`
FIELDER Samuel `-----1--------` / `-------------- 2 -`
FIFER Jacob `--1-----------` / `--1--2--1----- - -`
FIFER Jacob Jr `----1---------` / `----1--------- - -`
FIGHT James `1---1---------` / `1---1--------- - -`
FISHBACK Jane `---22---------` / `-1-1--1------- 5 -`
FISHER Hillory `11---1--------` / `1---1-------- 3 -`
FITZPATRICK James `---1----1-----` / `---1----1----`
FLORA George `11--1---------` / `1---1--------- - -`
FLORA Thomas `-1--1---------` / `21--1-------- - -`
FLORAH James `1----1--------` / `-1--1--------- - -`
FLORAH William `-1--1---------` / `1---1-------- - -`
FOREST Elizabeth `--1---1-------` / `1221-1------- - -`
FOSTER David `23---1--------` / `-----1------- 2 -`
FOSTER George R `2-1-1---------` / `-1-1--1----- 1 -`
FOSTER Henry `312-----1----` / `2311121------- 8 -`
FOSTER James `---------1---` / `-----1---1--- - -`
FOSTER James Jr `121-11--------` / `1---1-------- - -`

FOSTER Robert `1---1---------` / `2---1-------- - -`
FOULTON Samuel `-112--1-------` / `111--1---1--- - -`
FRANKLIN Frederick `222--1--------` / `1-1--1-------- - -`
FRANKLIN John `--1--------1--` / `-1------1----- - -`
FRYMAN Jacob `1-31-1--------` / `22---1-------- - -`
FRYMAN Peter `----1---------` / `1---1-------- - -`
FUGATE James `211--1--------` / `1---1-------- - -`
FUGATE James Sr `----2----1---` / `-------------- 1 -`
FUGATE John `111---1-------` / `111--1-------- - -`
FUGATE Reuben `---1-1--------` / `-12--1-------- - -`
FULLER Joseph `1211----1----` / `---1--1------- - -`
FURGERSON Henry `-11-----1----` / `-11341-------- - -`
GAFFIN Otho `--21--1-------` / `-2-1--1------- - -`
GAUNCE Martin `21---1--------` / `----1--------- - -`
GAUNCE Samuel `1---1---------` / `----1--------- - -`
GEOGHAGAN Michael `1--11-1-------` / `13211-1------- - -`
GEOGHAGAN Milton `----1---------` / `---2---------- 1 -`
GILEN john `1----1--------` / `11--1---1---- - -`
GILL Matilda `12------------` / `1----1-------- - -`
GIVANS James `----1---------` / `2---1--------- - -`
GIVINS John W `1---1---------` / `1----1-------- - -`
GLASSCOCK Claborn `1---1---------` / `----1--------- - -`
GLASSCOCK David `--------1-----` / `---1--1------- 3 -`
GLASSCOCK Jesse `1-------1-----` / `1----1-------- - -`
GLEN Moses `2-----1-------` / `11--11-------- 3 -`
GLEN Simeon `-------1------` / `-------1----- - -`
GODMAN William `-1-2--1-------` / `1112--1------- 2 -`
GONCE Rachel `--------------` / `12--1-1------- 1 -`
GONSE Geo `--111---1-----` / `---13--1------ - -`
GOODIN William `1---1---------` / `---1---------- - -`
GOODING Enoch `-211--1-------` / `1-12--1------- - -`
GOSE Benjamin `1---1---------` / `---1---------- - -`
GOSLIN Nathan `-11---1-------` / `-312---------- - -`

```
GRAVES Joseph H      -----1--------
                     -------------  9 -
GRAVES Wiliam B      -----1--------
                     -------------  - -
GRAY DAvid           --2--1--------
                     ---1-1-------  - -
GRAY Elijah          ----1--------
                     ----1-------  - -
GRAY Isaac           -1-1111------
                     -1-2-1------  - -
GRAY James           ---2--1------
                     --2-1-1-----  - -
GRAY Joseph          11--1--------
                     11---1--1----  6 -
GRAY Katharine       -1112--------
                     ---11-1-----  - -
GRAY Reuben          ----1--------
                     ----1-------  - -
GRAY Squire          1--11--------
                     1-11-1------  - -
GRAY William         11-1--1------
                     112--1------  - -
GRAY William Jr      121---------
                     1-11-1------  - -
GRAYHAM Samuel       -1--------1---
                     --11--1-----  - -
GREEN James          ---311--------
                     -------------  5 -
GREEN Zachariah      -111--1------
                     ---1--1-----  - -
GREEN Zachariah      -1111-1------
                     --1---1-----  - -
GREGORY Thomas       11----1------
                     1-1-1-------  - -
GREGS Hiram          1---1--------
                     ----1-------  - -
GRIFFITH Martin      --111-1------
                     22-1--1------  5 -
GRIMES Geo           2---1--------
                     1---11--1----  - -
GRIMES Nancy         1321---------
                     1----1------  - -
GRIMES William       ---2---1-----
                     --11--1-----  - -
HACKLEY William      -3----1------
                     1----1-------  2 -
HALE Benjamin        -1-11----1---
                     ---1---2-----  1 -
HALE Jeremiah        -1-1-31------
                     11---1-------  1 -
HALE John            --11----1---
                     1---1--1-----  5 -
HALE Samuel          ---2--1------
                     322--1--------  3 -
HALE William         -------1
                     --1--1------  2 -
HALL Elihu           --1---1------
                     -21-1------  - -
HALL James           1121--1------
                     -111--1-----  - -
HALL John            ---12--------
                     ---1---------  - -
HALL Moses           -----1--------
                     -1---1-------  1 -
HALL Robert E        -1---1-------
                     21--1--------  2 -

HALL Samuel          1--111--------
                     11--2---------  1 -
HAM Elizabeth        -----2--------
                     ---12--1------  - -
HAM John             -1241-1-------
                     1-1---1-------  - -
HAM John Sr          --111--1------
                     ---12---------  - -
HAM Katherine        -----11-------
                     --------1----  - -
HAM Michael          1-1--1--------
                     -2---1--------  - -
HAM Samuel           -----1--------
                     2--1----------  - -
HAM Samuel           22-----1------
                     -1---1--------  - -
HAM Thomas           1----1--------
                     1---1---------  - -
HAMILTON Elizabeth   --------1------
                     ----1---------  1 -
HAMILTON James       22-1--1-------
                     -121-1--------  - -
HAMILTON James       221--1--------
                     111--1--------  - -
HAMILTON John        1-----1-------
                     22---1--------  - -
HAMILTON John        212--1--------
                     1-1--2---1---  1 -
HAMILTON William     1---1---------
                     ----1--------  A -
HAMILTON William     -32--1--------
                     1----1--------  - -
HAMILTON William H   --113---------
                     -11-2-1-------  - -
HARBET John          22--1-1-------
                     12---1--------  - -
HARBET Polly         112----------
                     11---1--------  - -
HARBOUR Thomas       -142-1--------
                     3----1----1--  - -
HARDIN Richard       1----1--------
                     212---1-------  - -
HARDY Armsted        -11---1-------
                     --1--1--------  D -
HARNEY Elijah        2---1---------
                     --1-1---------  - -
HARNEY Samuel        --11---1------
                     -11--11-------  - -
HARNEY Sarah         ---2----------
                     --1----1------  - -
HARNEY Thomas        -----1--------
                     22--1---------  - -
HARRIS John          12-1--1-------
                     --11-1--------  3 -
HARRIS Titus         -------------
                     -------------  - 3
HARRIS Titus Jr      -------------
                     -------------  - 5
HARRISON John R      ----1---------
                     ----1--------  - -
HARTLEY William      -12--1--------
                     21---1--------  - -
HAWKINS Elijah       ----1---------
                     ---1---------  - -
HAWKINS Isaac        2-12--1-------
                     -2--11-------  5 -
```

```
HAWKINS Samuel        --1------1---
                      ----2---1--- - -
HAWKINS William       -311---1------
                      --11--1------ - -
HAWKINS William Jr    -3211----1---
                      111---1------ 2 -
HAYDEN Clea           -------------
                      ------------- - 3
HAYDEN Mary           ---1----------
                      --11---1------ 6 -
HAZE Walter           -122--1----
                      1111--2---- - -
HEDDLESTON Alexander  -1---1--------
                      ----2---1---- - -
HEDDLESTON David      ----------1---
                      -1-1----1--- - -
HEDDLESTON Hanes      --1--1---1---
                      2-111---1---- - -
HEDDLESTON James      11-----1------
                      111--1-------- - -
HENDERSON John        -121---1------
                      --1----1---- - -
HENDRICK Jacob        ------1
                      2-----1------ - -
HENDRICK Michael      1--111-1------
                      1-123--1---- - -
HENDRIX John          -12---1-------
                      -111--1------ - -
HENDRIX Levi          1---2---------
                      1-1-1-------- 2 -
HENRY Richard D       1---2--------
                      ---1--------- 8 -
HENSEY John           2-----1-------
                      12--1-------- - -
HENSON Henry          ------1
                      -------------- - -
HENTON James          ------1---------
                      1--1---------- - -
HERINGTON John        -121--1-------
                      1111--1------ - -
HERNDON James         1---2--1-----
                      1--1---1------ 1 -
HERNDON Thomas        ---11---1----
                      ---1---1----- - -
HIATT Betty           1221----------
                      -21---1------ 5 -
HIBLER John           12---1--------
                      121---1------
HILDRETH John         --1--1--------
                      -11--1------ 1 -
HILDRETH Sarah        --11----------
                      ---------1---- - -
HILDRETH William      1-1-1---------
                      ----1---------- - -
HILL Caty             3-1-----------
                      ------1------ - -
HILL John             -111---1------
                      ---2---1----- - -
HILL Otha             1-2--1--------
                      12--1--------- - -
HILLOCH James         -1-2---1-----
                      111---1------ - -
HINTON Martha         --------------
                      ---211-1----- - -
HINTON William        11---1--------
                      1-----1------ - -

HOFFMAN Henry         -----1--------
                      1---1--------- - -
HOFFMAN John R        ------1-----
                      ------------- - 8
HOFFMAN Peter         ----------1---
                      ----1---1---- 1 -
HOLLADAY Thomas       1----1--------
                      -21--1-------- 6 -
HOLLADAY William      2---1---------
                      ----2--------- 4 -
HOLLADAY Wm           2311----1----
                      1---11---1--- G -
HOLLER Joseph L       2----1--------
                      ----1--------- - -
HOLLER Mary M         -1111---------
                      --1--1------- - -
HOLLY William         ---11---------
                      -----1-------- - -
HOMES Daniel          -11---1-------
                      12-111-------- - -
HOOK William          21---1--------
                      -----1------- - -
HOPKINS Ephraim       -2--1---------
                      2-1-1--------- 2 -
HOPKINS Herod         -----1--------
                      1--1---------- - -
HOPKINS Isaac         22---1--------
                      1----1-------- - -
HOPKINS Josiah        121--1-----1-
                      2----1--------- - -
HOPKINS Joslin        3-1--1--------
                      -1---1-------- 3 -
HOPKINS Peter         --1--1--------
                      21---1-------- - -
HORNBACK Adam         ----2-11------
                      1---4---1---- 3 -
HOSTETTER John        1-2----1------
                      -2----1------ - -
HOW Amos              --11-1--------
                      --12---11--- - -
HOW Anna              -222---------
                      1-1---1------ 3 -
HOW Jonas             ----------1---
                      ----------1--- - -
HOWARD Massa          --3-3---------
                      ---1---1----- D -
HOWE Anna             -1311--------
                      -----1------- 2 -
HOWE Edward           1----1--------
                      1---1--------- 3 -
HOWE Samuel           --1-1---1----
                      -1----1------- - -
HOWSE John            2--11--1--1--
                      -111-1-------- - -
HOWSE Jonathan        21---1-------
                      -1--1--------- - -
HOWSE Richard         --1---1------
                      1111--1------- - -
HUGHES John           13--11--------
                      1-1--1-------- 6 -
HUGHES William        1-12---1-----
                      1211--1------ B -
HUGHS Geo             22--1---------
                      1---1--------- - -
HUGHS Greyson         -1---1--------
                      2---2--------- - -
```

HUGHS Isaac	-112-1--------	
	-----1--------	- -
HUGHS Jesse	211-1-1-------	
	-121----------	4 -
HUGHS John	1---1---------	
	-----1--------	- -
HUGHS Keturah	--------------	
	---1---1------	6 -
HUGHS Pratt	------1-------	
	-----1--------	1 -
HURLEY James	-1----1-------	
	-111--1-------	- -
HURLEY Lewis	--------------	
	--------------	- 5
HUTTSELL Jacob	11-1--1-------	
	11----1-------	- -
JACKSON John	1----1--------	
	-1--1---------	- -
JACKSON Polly	21--1---------	
	-111-1--------	
JAMES Alexander	1---1---------	
	---1----------	- -
JAMES John	--12-1-1------	
	-1112--1------	- -
JAMES Thomas	----1---------	
	---1----------	- -
JAMES William	1---1---------	
	2---1---------	- -
JAMESON Samuel	212--1--------	
	-2---1---1----	- -
JEFFERS Paul C	11-2-1--------	
	-1-111--------	5 -
JEWELL Allen	-3-2---1------	
	2-2---1-------	- -
JOHNSON Elizabeth	--111---------	
	---13--1------	2 -
JOHNSON Isabella	--121---------	
	-------1------	3 -
JOHNSON James	------1-------	
	1---1---------	- -
JOHNSON James	----------1---	
	--------1-----	- -
JOHNSON John	1---1---------	
	11--1---------	- -
JOHNSON John C	----1---------	
	1---1---------	3 -
JOHNSON Jonathan	-1-2--1-------	
	-------1------	2 -
JOHNSON Joshua	------1-------	
	21--1---------	2 -
JOHNSON Robert	----1---------	
	---1---1------	- -
JOHNSON Robt	--1-----1-----	
	--------------	- -
JOHNSON William	-11--1--------	
	--1--1--------	- -
JOLLY James	1----1--------	
	211--1--------	- -
JOLLY John	2--2----1-----	
	1--1-1--------	- -
JOLLY John	1121--1-------	
	-1---1--------	- -
JOLLY Thomas	1---1---------	
	21--1---------	- -
JONES Drury	--1-----1-----	
	-------1------	- -
JONES John	-1111-1-------	
	--11--1-------	- -
JONES Joshua	1-11--1-------	
	-1--11--------	4 -
JONES Lewis	--1----1------	
	-1111-1-------	
JONES Morgan	-1---1--------	
	232--1--------	- -
JONES Moses	----1--1------	
	---11---------	7 -
JONES Thomas	-11-----1-----	
	------1-------	8 -
JONES William	1----1--------	
	1---1---------	- -
JONES William	-------1------	
	--------------	6 -
JONES William	1--------1----	
	1---1---------	- -
JORDAN Samuel	--------------	
	--------------	- 3
JORDAN Samuel	1-----1-------	
	----1---------	- -
KEACH James	21---1--------	
	----1---------	1 -
KEITH John	---2-1--------	
	--------------	- -
KELLY William	----1---------	
	--------1-----	- -
KENNEDAY Andrew	1---1---------	
	1---1---------	- -
KENNEDAY Hannah	--------------	
	----2---1-----	- -
KENNEDAY James	1----1--------	
	2----1--------	- -
KENNEDAY Robert	--31---1------	
	---1---1------	- -
KENNEDAY William	-2---1--------	
	2---1---------	1 -
KENNY Eli	----1---------	
	----1---------	- -
KENNY John	----1---------	
	1---1---------	- -
KENTON William	421--1--------	
	2----1--------	2 -
KERNS Adam	112-11--------	
	2-1-1---------	2 -
KERNS Limson	----1--1------	
	---1---1------	- -
KERSEY Elisha	----11--------	
	2111-1--------	- -
KERSEY John	----2---------	
	1---1---------	- -
KERSEY John	----1---1-----	
	----31-1------	- -
KERSEY John Jr	11-----------	
	11--1---------	- -
KERSEY Thomas	1---1---------	
	----1---------	- -
KESADON James	-2--11--------	
	3121-1--------	- -
KILLUM Isaac	1---1---------	
	----1---------	- -
KILLUM Peter	--12---1------	
	-11-----1-----	- -
KIMBROW Geo W	2---1---------	
	1--11---------	- -

Name	Line 1	Line 2	Extra
KIMBROW Robert	---2--1--------	-----1--------	3 -
KIMBROW Sampson	--------------	--------------	- 4
KINCADE George	---2--1-----	--1-1-1-----	- -
KINCART John	-2---1--------	211--1--------	1 -
KING Richard	1-1--1--------	21--1--------	- -
KNOX Samuel	2211---1-----	-----1----1--	- -
KOOKENDOFFER Christian	321-1--------	-11-1--------	- -
LANE Thomas	1--11--------	--1----------	- -
LAWRENCE John	11---1-----	11---1-----	- -
LAWRENCE William	3112-1--------	11---1--------	- -
LEACH James G	2----11------	-2--1-1------	1 -
LEACH Tabitha	1--1----------	-2-1--1------	- -
LEAR Jacob	------1-----	------1-----	1
LEE Thomas R	--------1----	--------1----	- -
LEHR Alexander	21---1--------	----1--------	- -
LERNS Edward	---1----------	1--1----------	- -
LETTON Michel	-----3--1------	1--1----1-----	6 -
LEVENGOOD Philip	-1---1--------	-12--1--------	- -
LILLY Pleasant	-112---1-----	1-1-1-1------	
LINNBACK Abraham	-1---1--------	1-1--1---------	- -
LINSWELL Lewis	11-21--1------	2-11-1--------	- -
LINVILLE Jacob B	----1----------	1---1----------	- -
LOCHARD Jacob	----1--------	1-1--1--------	- -
LOCKRIDGE Rober	----1-1-------	11221-1-------	- -
LOCKRIDGE William	-1---1--------	211--1--------	- -
LOGAN Michael	-13--1--------	21-1-1---------	- -
LOGAN William	----1----------	----1----------	- -
LOGAN William Sr	-----------1---	---1--1-1----	- -
LOLLER Robt	11----1-------	1111--1-------	- -
LONG Eliahu	-122---1------	--1----1----	4 -
LONG James	1---1---------	----1---------	- -
LOUDERBACK Isaac	1---1---------	1---1---------	- -
LOW Isaac	----1---------	1---1---------	- -
LOW Isaac Sr	-1--------1---	-1--1---1----	- -
LOW Squire	1--1--------	1--1--------	- -
LYNN Timothy	------1-----	--211--------	- -
LYNN William	2-11---1------	-31111--------	- -
LYNVILLE John	-112---1-----	-1--21--------	- -
LYNVILLE John	1---1--------	1---1--------	- -
MADDOX Bazele	2---1--------	-1--1--------	- -
MADDOX Bennett	-11---1-----	1212--11------	
MADDOX Henley	-------1-----	-------1-----	D -
MADDOX James	----1--------	--1----------	- -
MAGNER Edward	-2---1--------	2----1--------	
MAGNER Mary	--11--------	----11--1----	- -
MAGNER William	1--21-1------	1121--1-------	- -
MAHN Briant	--------1----	----21-1------	7 -
MAIN Andrew	----1--------	2---1---------	
MAIRS Samuel	1-1---1------	2221-1--------	- -
MALLERY George	--------------	--------------	1 2
MALLERY John	31--1--1------	11---1--1-----	4 -
MANN Jacob	131--1--------	1---1---------	- -
MANN Jacob	1---1--------	1---1--------	- -
MANN John	----1--------	1---1---------	
MANN John Sr	12-21--1------	-2121--1------	- -
MANN Peter	--122--1------	-11-1-1-------	- -
MANNING Henry	1----1--------	-321-1--------	- -
MARSH Abraham C	-----1--------	1-----1-------	
MARSHALL Hugh	--2---1--------	-2-2--1--------	
MARTIN Edmund	121--1--------	--2--1--------	6 -
MARTIN James	223-1--1------	-1-2-1--------	
MARTIN John J	----1--------	----1---------	6 -
MARTIN John Sr	--------1---	-------1-----	- -
MARTIN Nehemiah	111-1--1-----	21113--------	- -
MASTON Caleb	1---1--------	13---2--------	- -
MASTON Peter	--------1----	--------------	4 -

Name	Census data
MASTON Peter G	`1---1--------` `1--1----- - -`
MATCHETT John	`---12--1-----` `1------1----- 4 -`
MATHERS Benjamin	`1---11---1---` `11--1-------- 1 -`
MATHERS Gavin	`--111-1------` `1211-1------- - -`
MATHERS James	`3-1---1------` `-1-1-1------- - -`
MATHERS Mary	`-1-----------` `21--1--------`
MATHERS Samuel	`1-1---1------` `1----1---1--- - -`
MATHERS Thomas	`----1----1---` `---1----1---- - -`
MATHERS Thomas	`1---1--------` `11--1-------- - -`
MATHERS William	`---21-1------` `-1---1------- 2 -`
MAUPIN Bennett	`21----1------` `---1--------- - -`
MAYBERRY John	`-------------` `------------- - 6`
MEDLIN John	`2----1-------` `-2--1-------- - -`
MEDLIN Richard	`1----1-------` `2--1--------- - -`
MEEKS James	`----1--------` `2--1----1--- - -`
MEEKS John	`-111-1-------` `12-1-1------- - -`
MENACH John	`1--1--1---1--` `211--1---1--- - -`
MENEFEE James	`1---1--------` `-1-1-1------- - -`
MENEFEE John	`1----1-------` `21--1-------- 3 -`
MENIFEE Jonas N	`-2----1------` `1---1-------- 2 -`
METCALFE Isabella	`-1---1-------` `11--1-------- 1 -`
MICHELL Joseph	`-1-11-1------` `1221--1------ 1 -`
MILES Amos	`1----1-------` `----1-------- - -`
MILLER James	`---1--1------` `-2121-1------ - -`
MILLER John	`---11-11-----` `-------1----- 4 -`
MILLER John A	`1-1------1---` `-1111--1----- - -`
MILLER Polly	`1--1---------` `-11-1-------- 1 -`
MILLER Samuel	`----1--------` `--1--------- - -`
MILLER William	`1---1--------` `1---1-------- 3 -`
MITCHELL Samuel	`3321-1-------` `--2--1------- - -`
MITCHELTREE John	`--1--1-------` `------1------ 4 -`
MOCHBY Nancy	`---2---------` `------1------ - -`
MOLER Elizabeth	`1-121--------` `-211--1------ - -`
MOLER Isaac Sr	`2-------1-----` `1211-1-------- - -`
MOLER John	`----1---------` `---1--------- - -`
MOLER John	`----1---------` `---1--------- - -`
MOLER Joseph	`------1-------` `12--11-------- - -`
MONFORD James	`-------------` `------------- - 2`
MONSON Samuel	`121--1--------` `--1--1------- 2 -`
MONSON Thomas	`11-1-1--------` `11--1-------- 1 -`
MOORE John H	`-1---1--------` `-21--1------- 1 -`
MOORE Thomas	`-2321-1-------` `2--2--1--1--- - -`
MORGAN John L	`1--111--------` `----1-------- 3 -`
MORGAN Joseph	`--------1-----` `------------- 4 -`
MORRIS Daniel C	`1111--1-------` `-1-1-1------- - -`
MORRIS Thomas	`21--1--------` `-1--1-------- - -`
MULLENS Seldon	`1---1--------` `----1-------- - -`
MULLICAN Benjamin	`1-1--1--------` `212--1------- - -`
MULLICAN Leonard	`----1--------` `-----1------- 1 -`
MULLICAN William Sr	`---12-1-------` `-1----1------ 5 -`
MURPHY George W	`-1121-11------` `12-2--1------- - -`
MUSGROVE Arpharad	`-----1--------` `---1--------- - -`
MUSGROVE Gilbert	`1---2---1-----` `-1------1---- 1 -`
MUSGROVE William	`-----1--------` `1--1--------- 3 -`
MUSICK Thomas	`--11-1--------` `------1------ 3 -`
MYERS Abraham	`121---1-------` `121-1-------- - -`
MYERS Daniel	`1-2---1-------` `12--1-------- - -`
MYERS David	`-12-----1-----` `---1--------- - -`
MYERS Geo	`22----1-------` `1----1------- - -`
MYERS Jacob	`----1--------` `11--1-------- - -`
MYERS John	`-2111--1------` `--211--1------ 9 -`
MYERS Lewis	`1212--1-------` `211--1------- - -`
MYERS Margaret	`---111--------` `----1----1--- - -`
MYERS Peter	`11-1-1--------` `1-2--1------- 1 -`
McANULTA Jane	`---2---------` `-------1------ - -`
McANULTA Joseph	`1---1--------` `1---1-------- - -`

Name	Census Data
McCABE James	-111--1------- 12---1--------- - -
McCABE Josiah	----2--------- 2--11--------- 1 -
McCARY Robt	1---1--------- 1----1------- - -
McCLANAHAM Elizabeth	--2-1--------- ---21--1----- - -
McCLANAHAN Charles	-1---1--------- 2--11----2--- - -
McCLANAHAN John	-----1--------- ----1--------- - -
McCLINTOCK Alexander	--1-1--------- --1--1--1----- 1 -
McCLINTOCK Hugh	----2----1---- ----3---1----- 1 -
McCLINTOCK John	-1--11--------- ----1--------- - -
McCLINTOCK William	12--1-1------- 1-2--1--------- 4 -
McCONNAHAY John	----------1---- ----11------- - -
McCONNAHAY John Jr	--111--------- ----1--------- - -
McCORD John H	1---1--------- 1---1--1------ - -
McCORD William	----1--------- 2---1--------- - -
McCORMICK John	1---11--------- ----1--------- 1 -
McCORMICK Walter	-----1--------- --1-11--------- - -
McCOY Mary	--11--------- ----31-1------ - -
McCUNE Gavin	-21--1--------- --12-1------- - -
McCUNE Hugh	-----1--------- 22--1--------- - -
McCUNE John	13---1--------- 2-1-1--------- - -
McCUNE John Jr	----1--------- 1---1--------- - -
McCUNE John M	1----1--------- 2---1--------- - -
McCUNE Joseph	----1--------- ----1--------- - -
McCUNE Robert	-2211-1------- ----2-1------- - -
McCUNE Robert	------2--------- --1-2--1------ - -
McCUNE Samuel	21----1------- 1-----1------- - -
McDANNAL Alexander	---1----1----- -1------1----- - -
McDANNAL Nehemiah	1--1--------- ----1--------- - -
McDANNEL Peter	-21----1----- -3-1-1--------- - -
McDANNEL Thomas	111--1--------- 211--1--------- - -
McDONALD Hugh	--2-2--1------ -11-1--1------ - -
McDONALD Lucy	------------- 1-1-2--------- - -
McDONALD Mordeci	---11---1----- ---1-1-1----- - -
McDONNEL John	2-1---1------- 1111--1------ - -
McDOWELL John B	-----1--------- 11211--------- - -
McDOWELL Robert	----1--------- 21--1--------- - -
McDOWELL Thomas	1----1--------- 13--1--------- - -
McGINNES Susannah	-211--------- ------1--------- -
McILVAIN John B	1----1--------- 1---1------- 2 -
McINTIRE James	-----1--------- 1---1--------- - -
McINTIRE James	--------1------- --1-----1----- - -
McMAHAN Andrew	----1--------- 1---1--------- - -
McMAHAN James	1----1--------- 2---1--------- - -
McMAHAN John	-----1--------- 2---1--------- 1 -
McMAHAN Robert	---2----1---- --1-1--1----- - -
McMAHAN Robt Jr	----1--------- 1---1------- - -
McMAHAN William	3------1------- -12--1--------- - -
McMICHAEL John	31122--1----- ---11-1------- - -
McMICHAEL William	1---1--------- ----1--------- - -
McQUOWN Lawrence	1----1--------- 2---1--------- - -
McVAY John	1-31-1------- 111--1--1---- - -
NEAL John	12-1-1------- 112--1--------- E -
NEAL Thomas	1----1--------- 1-1-1--------- 1 -
NEAL William	-----1--------- 1--1--------- 1 -
NELSON Moses	--12--1------- -1---1------- 1 -
NESBET David	1---2--------- ---1--------- 1 -
NESBIT Sarah	---1-1--------- --2--3---1---- - -
NEWMAN Augusta	311--1--------- -1-1---------
NEWMAN John	11---1--------- 11--1--------- - -
NICKERSON Isaac	1---2--------- ----1--------- - 1
NICKERSON Mary	------------- ----1--1------ - -
NICKERSON William	----1--------- ---1--------- - -
NOBLE Charles	-----1--------- ----11-------
NORTON Hiram	2--1-1------- 12--1--------- 6 -
OGDEN Enos	122----1----- -1-1-1------- - -
OGDEN Lucy	212--1--------- -1--1-1------ 5 -

Name	Census
OLIVER Robert	1----1-------- 2---1--------- - -
ONEAL Lewis	-111--1------ 111---1------ - -
ORMS Walter	----1-------- 1---1-------- - -
ORR John	111---1------ -11-1--1---- 2 -
OVERBY Henry	-2131-1------ -----1------ 6 -
OWINS John	-11---1------ 1111-1------- - -
OWINS Polly	1-11--------- 2-11--1----- - -
PADGETT Daniel	--11----1---- -1-1--1----- - -
PAINTER Solomon	--1--1------- 12---1------- - -
PALMER David	---12---1---- 1--13---1---- - -
PARAMON Isaac	-----1------- 1--1--------- - -
PARISH Bartlett	---2---1----- ------------ - -
PARISH David	21--1-------- -12--1---1--- 3 -
PARISH Jonithan	1----1------- 1----1------- - -
PARISH Opea	-------1------ ----1-------- - -
PARISH William	12------1----- 22---1------- - -
PARKER Charles	2-114--1----- -21--11------ A -
PARKER Peter	--11--1------ --1---------- - -
PARKER Solomon	122---1------ 2---1-------- - -
PARKS James	2----1--1---- ----1------- 3 -
PARKS James Jr	----11------- ------------ 1 -
PARKS Joseph	1----1------- --1-1-------- 1 -
PARSONS Josiah	----1-------- ----1------- - -
PATTEN Alexander	----1-------- ---1-------- - -
PATTEN John	2---2-------- -1--1-------- 4 -
PATTEN Thomas R	111---1------ 2-21--------- 2 -
PAULEY Jeremiah	2-11--1------ -111-1------- - -
PAULEY William	--11---1----- --21--1------ - -
PAULEY Zachariah	311--1------- -11--1------- - -
PAXTON Robt	-1-12---1---- ---1--1----- - -
PAYNE Berry	--11--1------ ----21-1----- - -
PAYNE Robt	111--1------- 11---1-1----- C -
PAYTON Joseph	----1-------- 11--1-------- - -
PAYTON William	111-21------- 3211-1------- - -
PEEPLES John	111--1------- 21---1------- 2
PEYTON Stephen	--122---1---- -1--11-1----- - -
PEYTON William	-1--11-1----- 21---1------- -
PIPER James	---11-1------ --1---1------ 7 -
PIPER John	1---1-------- 1---1-------- 1 -
PIPER John	2---1-------- --1--------- 2 -
PIPER Robert	--111--1----- -1-1--1------ - -
PIPER Samuel	1---1-------- ----1------- 2 -
PIPER Samuel	----1--1----- --1---1------ 3 -
PLANK Michel	--111--1----- --1---1------ - -
PLUE Elias	-----1------- 3---1-------- - -
PLUE Elias Sr	2-2-----1---- -1-----1----- - -
POISAL James	--1-1-------- --11--1------ - -
POLLOCK James	1111----1---- -1----1------ 3 -
POTTS Henry	22-1-1------- --1-1-------- 2 -
POTTS James	1--1-1------- 22--1-------- 2 -
POTTS John	1------1----- -123-1------- - -
POTTS William	1---1-------- ---11---1---- 4 1
POWELL Isaac	112---1------ 22-2-1------- - -
POWELL Jeremiah	1-12--1------ -111-1------- 1 -
POWELL John	1121---1----- ---1-1------- - -
POWELL Nathan	-1---1------- 1---1-------- - -
POWELL Robt	123--1------- 1----1------- - -
PRATHER Barret	--122--1----- -11-1--1----- 5 -
PRATHER Benjamin	-12---1------ 2----1------- 2 -
PRATHER Thomas	----2--1----- ----2--1----- - -
PRICE Joseph	11---1------- 11---1------- - -
QUIET James	--1--11------ --1--1------- - -
RAFFERDAY Joseph	112--1------- 22---1------- - -
RAMEY William C	21---1------- -----1------- - -
RANKIN Clement	1---1-------- 1---1-------- - -
RANKINS John	21-1---1----- -2-1--1------ - -

NICHOLAS COUNTY KENTUCKY 1830 CENSUS

Name	Line 1	Line 2
RANKINS Moses	--------1----	--12---1------ 2 -
RANKINS Robert	-----1--------	---1--------- - -
RAY John	--------1----	-------1----- - 1
REAS Jeremiah	----5--------	-----1------- 1 -
REED James	11---1-------	112--1------- - -
REVEAL Joseph	----1--1-----	--11---1------ 1 -
RIBELIN Martin	----1---1----	---1---1------ - -
RICHARD William	212---1------	---1-1--1---- - -
RICHARDS Andrew	31---1-------	--1--1------- - -
RICHARDSON James	1--1----1----	121--1------- - -
RICKETS William	----1--------	2---1-------- - -
RIGGINS Jesse	---------1----	----1--1------ - -
RIGGS Clement	--222--1------	-311---1------ - -
RIGGS Erasmus	--2--1--1----	-223-1-1------ 7 -
RIGGS John W	1----1--------	2--1---------- 1 -
RILEY John	-1--------1----	-2--2--1------ - -
RILEY John Jr	-----1--------	1--1---------- - -
RITCHEY Asa	1122--1------	----2-1------- - -
RITCHEY Henry	111--1--------	2211--1------- - -
RITCHEY Isaac	-----1---------	---1----1------ - -
RITCHEY John	----1---------	1--1---------- - -
RITCHEY Solomon	21-2--1-------	111---1------- - -
RITCHEY William	-2---1--------	21--1--------- - -
RITCHEY William Jr	2----1--------	1---1--------- - -
RITCHEY Zachariah	21---1--------	-13-1--------- - -
ROBERTS Henly	-1-14--1------	11--1-1------- - -
ROBERTS Isabella	-2------------	-1---1-------- - -
ROBERTS Thomas	--------1------	--22---1------ - -
ROBINS Spencer	1------1-------	-1---1-------- 2 -
ROBINSON David	22---1--------	11---1-------- - -
ROBINSON Isaac	12--1---------	1---1---1----- - -
ROBINSON John	----1--1------	-13---1------- - -
ROBINSON Mary	--------------	--------1----- 5 -
ROBINSON Nathaniel	-1--11--------	-21--1-1------ 4 -
ROBINSON Samuel	----11----1--	-1---1---1--- - -
ROBINSON Stephen	----------1---	-------------- - -
ROBY Levan	----2--------	1--1---------- - -
RODES Samuel E	111---1------	-1--1-------- - -
ROGERS James T	----1--------	--1--1------- - -
ROGERS John	11--1--------	1---1-------- - -
ROGERS John	1---1--------	--1-1-------- - -
ROGERS John	11--1--------	2---1-------- - -
ROGERS Willis	1--1----------	-------------- - -
ROLLINS Henry	1--1----------	-------------- - 1
ROLSTON John	1---1--------	1---1-------- - -
ROLSTON Robert	-------1------	-------1------ - -
ROSS Greenberry	3-22-2-------	----2-------- 1 -
ROSS John	--1----1-----	-111---1------ - -
ROSS John Jr	-----1--------	1--1---------- - -
ROSS Joseph	-----1--------	221--1-------- - -
ROSS Philip	----1--------	3-----1-1------ - -
ROSS Stephen	----1--------	----1--------- - -
ROSS Thomas	1----1--------	211-1-------- 2 -
ROSS Tilman	----2--2------	----1--1------ - -
ROSSER Mahala	21------------	--1-1--------- - -
ROYSE Hiram	11-2--1-1-----	-12---1------ - -
ROYSE Solomon	---1-1--------	-11-1-------- 6 -
ROYSE William	1111---1-----	1111-1-1------ - -
RUDDLE George W	11----1-------	-111-1-------- 8 -
RUDDLE William	--------1------	---1--11----- 3 -
RUNNELS Polly	--2-----------	----1--------- - -
RUSSELL Wm H	21--1---------	----1--1------ 5 -
SADLER Edward	---1--1-------	--1-11-1------ - -
SAMPLE James	2--1----------	----1--------- - -
SANDERS John	-2--2---1-----	31--2---1----- - -
SAVITEER William	1--1-1--------	221111-------- - -

SCONCE David L
-2--1---------
1---1--------- - -

SCONCE Henry
----1---------
----1---1---- - -

SCOTT Andrew
----1---------
1--1--------- - -

SCOTT Elijah
21---1--------
1---1-------- - -

SCOTT Elijah
122--1--------
11---1------- - -

SCOTT John C
1-1-1---------
-1-1--1------ - -

SCOTT Josiah
-1-----1------
--11--1------ 1 -

SCOTT Nathaniel
1-----1-------
212--1-------- - -

SCOTT Thomas
-11----1------
-222--1------- - -

SCOTT William C
1---1---------
---1--------- - -

SEARS Elizabeth
--121---------
-2---1------- - -

SEARS James
3---1---------
----1-------- - -

SEARS Michael
111--1--------
11--1-------- - -

SECREST William
--11-1--------
--1-1-------- 3 -

SELBY Barley
--112-1-------
221-11------- - -

SELBY Henry
1--1--1-------
1312-1-------- - -

SELBY Majour
---------1---
---------1--- - -

SHAFFER John
1----1--------
1111-1------- - -

SHANKLIN Andrew
----1---------
2--11-------- - -

SHANKLIN Benjamin
1-1---1-------
-2----1------ - -

SHANKLIN James H
1---1---------
1---1-------- - -

SHANKLIN John W
2---1---------
11--1-------- - -

SHANKLIN Johnsen
---------1----
-1-------1--- - -

SHANKLIN William J
----1---------
1--11--1----- - -

SHANKS David
--11----1----
---21--1----- - -

SHANNON Jeremiah
21---1--------
-1-1--------- - -

SHANNON Robert
1---1---------
----1-------- 1 -

SHANNON Samuel
11-1--1-------
111--1-------- - -

SHAW Geo
1-1--1--------
2---1-------- - -

SHAW Lewis
11---1--------
3-2-1-------- - -

SHAW Pricilla
---1----------
--------11--- - -

SHELEY David
-21---1-------
1----1-------- - -

SHOULTS Henry
11-1-1--------
-22--1-------- - -

SHOULTS John B
3-1-1---------
---21-111---- - -

SHRIOCK Daniel
1----1--------
----1-------- - -

SHROWSBY Samuel
-1--1---------
1----11------ - -

SIMMS Ambros
122-11--------
111--1------- 5 -

SKIDMORE Michael
1---1---------
--1---------- - -

SLED Sarah
--11----------
-------1----- 3 -

SLOOP Margaret
----1---------
--------1---- - -

SLOOP Moses
----1---------
--1---------- - -

SLOOP William
-1---1--------
2---1-------- - -

SMALL James
--212--1------
-------1--1-- 1 -

SMART Elijah
2----1--------
----1-------- - -

SMART Humphrey
1121--1-------
12-1--1------ - -

SMART Samuel
11----1-------
1-----1------ 1 -

SMART William
2----1--------
----1-------- - -

SMEDLEY Aron
1----1--------
11--1-------- 5 -

SMILEY Polly
22------------
--2--1------- - -

SMITH Andrew
----1---------
----1-------- - -

SMITH James
--2-----1----
--11---1----- - -

SMITH James
----1---------
------------- 2 -

SMITH Jetson
1-1-1---------
1---1-------- - -

SMITH John
--11--1-------
-1111-1------ - -

SMITH Joseph
1---1---------
1---1-------- - -

SMITH Letton
---11---------
1---1-------- 1 -

SMITH Mitchell
--11---1------
--11---1----- - -

SMITH Nathan
221--1--------
-1---1-------- - -

SMITH Patterson
121--1--------
12---1--1---- - -

SMITH Robert
----1---------
--1---------- - -

SMITH Samuel
--112---------
-------1----- 4 -

SMITH Samuel M
---111--------
---1-1-------- L -

SMITH William
1-----1---1--
2----1--1---- - -

SMITH William
----2---------
----2-------- - -

SMITHERS John
1---1---------
2---1-------- 3 -

SNAP Daniel
--11--1-------
-11---------- - -

Name	Census marks
SNAP Elijah	21--1--------- -1--1--------- - -
SNAP Jacob	2----1------- ----1--------- - -
SNAP Peggy	-1----------- 11---1------- - -
SNAP Peter	1---1------- 1---1--------- - -
SNAP Peter	----------1--- ----------1--- - -
SNAP Sally	-212--------- ----1-1------ - -
SNAP Samuel	--1----1----- --1--1------- - -
SOWSBY Philip	--2---1------ -2-1--1------ - -
SOWSBY Robert	--11--------- 1--1--------- - -
SOWSBY Thomas	121--1------- 1---1--------- - -
SOWSBY Thomas	----1--1------ -------1----- - -
SPARKS Edward	1---1--------- ----1--------- - -
SPARKS George	--111--1----- 111---1------
SPARKS Jonas	2---11------- -1--1-------- - -
SPARKS Katherine	------------- -1111---1---- - -
SPARKS William	-1---1------- 12---1--1---- - -
SPEEDLE John	---------1---- -1---1------- - -
SPENCER James	------1------ --1--1------- - -
SPHAR Henry	--1----1----- --121--2----- - -
SQUIRES James	-----1------- 1---1------- 3 -
SQUIRES John M	------1------ 1---1------- 3 -
SQUIRES Leonard	2---1-------- 1---1------- 1 -
SQUIRES Margaret	--111-------- --1----1------ 1 -
STADLEY John	--------1----- --111-------- - -
STADLEY William	2-----1------ ------1------ - -
STANDIFORD James	231---1------- -1-2--1------- - -
STANDIFORD John	-------1------ ------------- 1 -
STARK James	1---1-------- 11--1-------- - -
STEEL Samuel H	-2---1------- 3--11-------- 3 -
STEPHENSON Ann	-1-1--------- --1--1---- - -
STEPHENSON George	-1------1----- ---------1----- - -
STEPHENSON John	21---1------- 2--1------- - -
STEPHENSON John	1---11------- 3--1--------- - -
STEPHENSON Joseph	--23--1------ ----1-1------- - -
STEPHENSON Robert	2---1------- ----1--------- - -
STEPHENSON Robert	-111--1------ 22----1------ - -
STEPHENSON Robert Sr	2-22--1------ -1----1------- - -
STEPHENSON Thomas M	------1------ 111-1-1------ 6 -
STEPHENSON William	1111---1----- 11-1-1------- - -
STEWART Abel	-------1------ -------1------ - -
STEWART William	--1---1------ ---11-1------- - -
STEWART William	1---1------- 1---1------- - -
STITT James	111--1------- 11--1-------- 1 -
STITT Polly	---11--------- --------1---- 1 -
STOGDEN John B	1221--------- 1--1--1----- 1 -
STOKER Edward	--11--1------ --11--1------ - -
STOKER Joseph	------1------- --11--1------ - -
STOKER William	1-----1------ 1-----1------ - -
STOKES John	2----1------- -23--2--1---- - -
STOKES Thomas	2----1------- 12--1--------- - -
STONE William	1-1-1-------- 1--1-------- - -
STOOPS James	-11--1------- 311--1------- - -
STOOPS John	1221--1------ 2-1-1--------- - -
STOOPS Sarah	--111--------- -11--1------- - -
STOOPS William Sr	22---1------- -13--1------- - -
STORY Permelia	--1---------- 121--1------- - -
STOUT Oliver H	1----1------- ----1------- 1 -
SUDDITH John	-222--1------ 31---1------- 1 -
SUMMERS Archibald	1--11-11----- -2112-2--1--- 1 -
SUMMETT Elijah	1-1--1------- 2---1-------- - -
SUMMETT Geo	--1----1---- 2--11---1---- 1 -
SUMMETT Jacob	1---1-------- 11--1-------- - -
SUMMETT James	11---1------- 12--1-------- - -
SUMMETT WAlter W	1--21-1------ -1-1--1------ - -
SWAIN James	21----1------ ---21-1------- - -
SWART George	11---1------- 22---1------- 1 -

Name	Line 1	Line 2	
SWART Margaret	---11---------	----1--1------	1 -
TANNER Richard	2213---1-----	1111-1-------	- -
TARR Charles	---1------1---	--11--1------	8 -
TARR John	21--1--------	1---1-------	1 -
TAYLOR Betsy	-11----------	-11--1-------	- -
TAYLOR George	1--1--1------	111-11-------	- -
TAYLOR John	1-1-1--1-----	-12-1-1------	- -
TAYLOR John	11----1------	2111-1-------	- -
TAYLOR Rebecca	1---1--------	--111--1-----	- -
TERRY Reuben	---1----1----	----------1---	3 -
THACKER Berry	2-1-1--------	12--1--------	- -
THACKER John	31---1-------	-1---1-------	- -
THOMAS Augusta	----1--------	1--1---------	- -
THOMAS Daniel	---11-1------	-111--1------	- -
THOMAS James	3----1-------	----1--------	2 -
THOMAS James	13--1-1------	1----11------	3 -
THOMAS John L	111--1-------	211-1-1------	- -
THOMAS Lydia	-122---------	---21--1-----	7 -
THOMASON Abner	1----1-------	2---1--------	- -
THOMASON Landy	---1---1-----	--12---1-----	- -
THOMPSON James A	11--31-------	1---1--1-----	- -
THROCKMORTON Aris	-211--1------	1-1--1-------	L -
THROCKMORTON Jno	-111---1-----	-1111-1------	B -
THROCKMORTON John J	----1--------	--1----------	1 -
THROCKMORTON Tho Sr	-22----1-----	--12---1-----	9 -
THROCKMORTON Thomas R	1---1--------	2---1--------	6 -
TINNY James	11-111-------	----1--------	- -
TINNY John	----1--------	---1----1----	- -
TRIGG Ezekiel	----1--------	----1--------	- -
TRIGG John	1----1-------	1---1--------	- -
TRIGG Thomas	---11---1----	----11--1----	- -
TROUTMAN Geo	-1---1-------	2---11-------	- -
TUCKER Samuel	-12---1------	12-1--1------	- -
TULL Jesse	1---1--------	---1---------	- -
TULL John	--31--1------	21-2--1--1---	1 -
TUNE Samuel	----1--------	--------1----	5 -
TUREMAN Charles	---11--------	1--1--------	4 -
TUREMAN Joseph F	1---11-------	11---1-------	4 -
TUREMAN Valentine	---1-----1---	--1-1--1-----	- -
TURLEY John	12---1-------	2-1-1--------	2 2
TURLEY Sampson	-------------	-------------	- 2
TURNER Larkin	1---1--------	---1---------	- -
TWEDY David	-------1-----	1-311--1-----	- -
UTTERBACK Harmon	---------1---	-------1-----	- -
VANDERLIN Stephen	2---11-------	-21--1-------	4 -
VANSCHOICK Hezekiah	--111--1-----	-212-11------	- 1
VANSCHOICK Josiah	12-1-11------	--12-1-------	- -
VAUGHN James	12---1-------	111-1-1------	1 -
VEACH Ambrose	-1--1--------	----1--------	1 -
VEACH Kelly	-------------	1---1--------	- -
VICTOR Ambrose D	1---1--------	---1---------	- -
VICTOR John	1-11-1-------	111--1-------	3 -
VICTOR Nancy	--1----------	-1---2--1----	B -
VICTOR William	2-221--1-----	--1---1------	3 -
VIMOUNT Franklin D	1---2--------	1---1--------	5 -
WADDLE Joseph	222---1------	1--22--------	- -
WAGGONER Geo	21---1-------	-1-1---------	- -
WAGGONER John	21---1-------	----1--------	- -
WALL Reuben	--1-----1---	----1----1---	- -
WALL Zachariah	2----1-------	1---1--------	- -
WALLIS John	2----1-------	-21-1--------	- -
WALLIS Sarah	----3--------	--------1----	- -
WARD Solomon	-3----1------	2---1-------	2 -
WARD William	1----1-------	132--1-------	- -
WARDLOW Joseph	---11-1------	-----2-------	2 -
WARMSLEY John W	----1--------	--11---------	- -

```
WASSON John          -----1---------
                     ---1--------- - -
WATSON John          ---------1-----
                     ---111-1------ - -
WATTS Francis        -1---1--------
                     1-1--1-------- - -
WAUGH Archer         -1--1--------
                     21--1--------- 1 -
WAUGH Samuel M       ---11--------
                     --1-1--------- 5 -
WEAVER Cornelius     1121--1-------
                     111-1--------- - -
WEAVER Peter         2211-1--------
                     111----1------ - -
WEBB Charles         -111---1------
                     -1-2--1------- - -
WELLS Nathan         --1-11--------
                     22311--------- - -
WELLS Ruth           --11---------
                     ----1-1------- - -
WELLS William        2----1--------
                     -----1------- - -
WEST Adam            -1---1--------
                     32--1--------- - -
WEST Amos            --11---1------
                     -111--1------- 4 -
WEST Elijah          ---11---------
                     1--1---------- 1 1
WEST Elijah          2111--1-------
                     -11-1--------- 2 -
WEST Philip          -1----1-------
                     --22-1-------- - -
WEST Robert          -----1---1----
                     -1---1-------- - -
WETHERFORD Jonas     -12--1--------
                     12---12------- - -
WHALEY Hiram         ----1---------
                     ----1--------- - -
WHALEY James         1---1---------
                     11--1--------- - -
WHALEY John          ----2-11------
                     --------1----- - -
WHEATLY Thomas       3----2---1----
                     -----1-------- 2 -
WHEELER Rebecca      -122----------
                     --1----1------ - -
WHEELER Samuel       --1---1-------
                     122--1-------- - -
WHEELER William      -111-----1----
                     ---2--1------- - -
WHISNER Jacob        -11--1--------
                     -11--11------- 1 -
WHITAKER James       11--1-1-------
                     -211--1------- - -
WHITE Lewis          1---1---------
                     ---1--------- - -
WHORTON Eli          --1----1-----
                     -1-1----1---- - -
WHORTON John         2---1---------
                     -1--1--------- - -
WIGGINS Archibald    -2----1-------
                     31---1-------- 1
WIGGINS Neal         -1---1--------
                     2---1--------- - -
WIGGINS Sarah        --1----------
                     ---------1---- 1 1

WIGGINS William      21------1-----
                     -12--1-------- 1 -
WILEY Hugh           -121--11-----
                     22111-1------- - -
WILLET Silas         11---1--------
                     -1--1--------- 3 -
WILLIAMS Elizabeth   ---1---------
                     ---1---1----- - -
WILLIAMS James       1----1--------
                     11--1--------- - -
WILLIAMS John        1---2---1-----
                     ---11--1----- - -
WILLIAMS John Jr     ----1--------
                     ---1--------- - -
WILLIAMS Mourton G   ----1---------
                     ---11-------- - -
WILLIAMS Samuel      13---1--------
                     1---1--------- 5 -
WILLIAMS William     111---1-------
                     1211-1-------- 3 -
WILLOW Jesse         --1---1-------
                     -------1------ - -
WILLS David          --12---1------
                     1--11--1------ - -
WILSON Charles       --111---------
                     ---1--1------- 3 -
WILSON David         211--1--------
                     111--1-------- - -
WILSON Jacob         ----1---------
                     1---1--------- - -
WILSON John          -----1--------
                     ----1--------- 1 -
WILSON John          ---1---------
                     ----1--------- - -
WILSON John          --11--1-------
                     ----1--1---1- - -
WILSON John          --21--1-------
                     -----1-1------ - -
WILSON Katharine     -------------
                     ----2----1---- - -
WILSON Michael       ----1---------
                     1--1---------- - -
WILSON Samuel        ----1---------
                     ---1--------- - -
WILSON Stephen       1221--1-------
                     -1----1------- - -
WILSON Thomas        -111--1-------
                     2121-1-------- - -
WOOD Geo             --1----11----
                     -------1------ - -
WOOD Jeremiah        12---1--------
                     11---1-------- 4 -
WOOD John            ---------1----
                     2---1--------- 7 -
WOOD Thomas          -11--1--------
                     2----1-------- - -
WOOD Wiliam          1312--1-------
                     --1--11------- - 1
WOODS David          1---1---------
                     2---1--------- - -
WOODS Joseph         12-1--1-------
                     1-31-11------- - -
WORKMAN Michael      2--11---------
                     1--11--------- - -
YATES Joal           ---11---------
                     1---1--------- - -
```

```
YOUNG Whittinton        ----1---------
                        ------------- 1 -
YOUNGER Joshua          1---1----1---
                        --1-1---1---- - -
YOUNGER Lewis           2--11---------
                        ----1--------- - -
```

ADAIR Juliann	---21---------	
	----1--1------ 1 -	
ADAIR Richard	11-2---1-----	
	122---1------ - -	
ADAMS Abigail	-11---------	
	---1--1------ - -	
ADAMS Jacob *	----2-------	
	---1--------- - -	
ADKINS Mary	---1---------	
	---1--1------ - -	
ADKINS Thomas	1111---1--1--	
	11212--1----- 1 -	
ADKINS Wisdom	2---1---------	
	----1--------- - -	
AINSWORTH Charles	---1---1-----	
	---1-1------- - -	
AIRS Thomas	---2-----1---	
	--2---1------- - -	
ALEXANDER David	1---1---------	
	----1--------- - -	
ALEXANDER George	1----1--------	
	111--1------- - -	
ALEXANDER Hiram	3----1--------	
	-----1-------- - -	
ALEXANDER James	--2---1-------	
	--1--1------- - -	
ALEXANDER Jesse	--1-----1-----	
	--1---1------- - -	
ALEXANDER Jesse	1---1---------	
	----1--------- - -	
ALEXANDER John	-1-2--1-------	
	-222--1------- - -	
ALEXANDER Thomas	-------1------	
	-11---1------ - -	
ALEXANDER William	1---2---------	
	----1-1------- - -	
ALLEN David	--21--1-------	
	3-1--2--------- 3 -	
ALLEN Granville	---11--1------	
	---1---1------ D -	
ALLEN Jesse	2132--1-------	
	-----1-------- - -	
ALLEN John C	----1---------	
	1---1--------- - -	
ALLEN Richard	22--1---------	
	-2--1--------- - -	
ALLENDER Thomas	22--1--------	
	1----1------- - -	
ALLISON David	11--1---------	
	22--1--------- - 1	
ALLISON Isaac	----1---------	
	2---1--1------ - -	
ALLISON James	12--1---------	
	1----1------- - -	
ANDERSON Alexander	-----1--------	
	-----1-------- - -	
ANDERSON Daniel	1-1-1---------	
	-12-1-1------- 1 -	
ANDERSON James	121--1--------	
	-1--1--------- - -	
ANDERSON Samuel	2------1-------	
	-1--1--------- 6 -	
ANDERSON Sarah	-1-----------	
	-111-1--1----- - -	
ANDERSON William	-1--1---------	
	----11--------- - -	
ARDRY Robert	---1---1-----	
	---1--1--1--- - -	
ARMS Walter	-----1-------	
	221-1--------- - -	
ARNETT SAmuel	----1---1----	
	----1---1---- 8 -	
ARNETT Thomas	2-1-11--------	
	-----1--------- 1 -	
ARNETT William	-1---1-------	
	1---1--------- - -	
ARNOLD James	-1-1--1------	
	--12-1------- - -	
ARNOLD John	1---1-------	
	-1---1------- - -	
ARNOLD Lewis H	---11---1----	
	---11------- 9 -	
ASBERRY Jeremiah	1----1------	
	2---1-------- 2 -	
ASHBROOK Andrew	-112--1------	
	-1111-1------- - -	
ASHBROOK Munson	2------------	
	1---1--------- 2 -	
ASHCRAFT Ephraim	----------1---	
	---------1---- - -	
ASHCROFT William E	-11---1------	
	232--1------- - -	
ASHLEY James P *	----1---1----	
	------------- 3 -	
ASHPAW Joseph	3----1-------	
	-1--1--------- - -	
ATKINSON William	-22---1-------	
	1-13--1------- 1 -	
BAILEY Elisha	-----1-------	
	12--1--------- 4 -	
BALL Fantly	-------1------	
	-------1------ - 2	
BALL John S	1211--1-------	
	1-11-1----1-- 1 -	
BALLENGALL Frances	----32-------	
	---11-1------- 4 -	
BALLENGALL Neil	11---1-------	
	11---1------- 8 -	
BANISTER John	----1-1------	
	--211-1------- - -	
BANTA Abraham	-2--12-------	
	111--1--------- - -	
BARLOW James	----1---------	
	----1--------- - -	
BARLOW John	----2---1----	
	---13--1------ 1 -	
BARLOW John	--13---1------	
	121---1------- - -	
BARLOW Joshua	----1---------	
	----1--------- - -	
BARLOW Leason	12-1-1--------	
	1-2--1--------- - -	
BARNETT James	--2--1-------	
	2-1--1--------- - -	
BARNETT James	21-1-1--1----	
	1---1--------- - -	
BARNETT James P	--2--1-------	
	111--11--1--- - -	
BARNETT John T	--1-2--1-----	
	--111--1------ - -	
BARNETT William	-111--1-------	
	--2---1------- - -	

Name	Tally
BARR Daniel	----1-------- ----1-------- - -
BARR Robert	-1-21----1---- -12---1------ - -
BARR Robert W	1---1-------- ----1------ - -
BARTLETT Samuel	----1---1---- --------1---- - -
BARTLETT Silas	1----1-------- 1---2-------- - -
BASKETT Charlotte	--11-------- --21--------- 2 -
BASKETT Hannah	--1---------- -11--1------- - -
BAXTER George	-----1------- -----11------- - -
BEARD Elizabeth	------------- -2-11-1------- 5 -
BECK William	--2---1------- -------1----- 4 -
BECKERER Jacob L	--1-1-1------- 1--2-1-------- 6 -
BECKNER Peter	211--1------- -1---11------- - -
BEDINGER George M	---1--1------- -------1------ 9 -
BEDINGER Joseph	-----1------- 1---1--------- - -
BELL John	--1--1------- 11-1-1------- - -
BELL Lawson	-211--1------- -1-3--1------- 1 -
BELL Loyd	22---1------- -11--1------- - -
BELL Moses	11---1------- -2-11--------- - 1
BELL William	--1------1---- -3----21-1---- - -
BELLIS Philip	1113--1------- 11--1-1------- - -
BENSON James	----2--------- 1-1-1--------- 2 -
BERKSHIRE Greenberry	----1-------- 1--1--------- - -
BERRY Francis	-11---1------- --1---1------- - -
BERRY George	--11-----1--- ---2---1----- - -
BERRY George M	1---1-------- --1---------- - -
BERRY Jesse	-212-1------- 111-1-------- - 1
BERRY Robert	--2-1----1--- ---1--1------ 5 -
BERRY Samuel	-----1------- 1---1-------- - -
BESHEARS Elijah	1---1-------- 12--1-------- - -
BISHOP Charles	1-1---1------- 11-11-------- - -
BISHOP Joseph	----1-------- 1---1-------- 1 -
BISHOP Joseph	--21--1------- 1---1-------- 6 -
BISHOP Josiah	---11--1------ --12--1------- - -
BISHOP Newton	-----1------- 1----1------- - -
BLACK Christopher	1---1-------- -3--1-------- - -
BLACK Matthew D	2--1-------- ----1------- - -
BLACK Samuel	2-2--1------- -2---1------- - -
BLACK Thomas	----1-------- -----1------- - -
BLACKAMORE Thomas	-11--1------- 1-1--1------- 1 -
BLACKBURN Joseph	---1--1------ -1-----1----- - -
BLAIR Alexander Jr	----1-1------ -----2------- - -
BLAIR Alexander Jr	----------1--- --------1-1--- 3 -
BLAIR James B	---11-1------ 23---1------- 4 -
BLUNT Hezekiah	-211--1------- 21-11-1------- - -
BLUNT William	2111--1------- 2-111--------- - -
BOARDMAN Abner	1-1--1--1---- -211-1--1---- D -
BOARDMAN James	-221--1------- ---1--------- 3 -
BOATMAN George	1----11------ 131--1--1---- - -
BOND Thomas E	121--1------- 11--1-1------- - -
BOON Deerbourn	1---1------- ----1------- - -
BOSLEY Elijah	-----1------- 2-1--1------- - -
BOSLEY Mary	2-1--------- -12--1------- - -
BOWAN Cajaby	21--1-------- 111-1-------- - -
BOWAN Isaac	11--1-------- 2--11--------- - -
BOWEN James	-11--1------- 221--1-------- - -
BOWEN William	--1--1----1-- 12--1-------- - -
BOWERS Robert	---111------- 111--1------- - -
BOWLS Hughes D	-----1------- 31--1-------- - -
BOWLS Powhattan	----1-------- 11--1-------- - -
BOYK John H	---------1--- ------------- - -
BRADLEY Darius	-----1------- 2---1-------- - -
BRADLEY Francis	3---1-------- ----1-------- - -
BRADLEY George Jr	1---1---1---- 1---1--1----- - -
BRADLEY George L	1-----1---1-- 1----1-------- - -
BRADLEY George W	----1-------- 1--1--------- - -
BRADSHAW Alexander	111--1----1-- -12---1------- - -

BRADY Hilton	21--1---------		BUCHANON James	-2211-1------	
	-1--1--------- - -			---12--------- 4 -	
BRADY Patrick	---11---1----		BUCKLER Robert	----4--------	
	--1122-1----- - -			------------- 1 -	
BRADY William	11----1------		BUCKLER Wilson	2--1---1-----	
	---1-1-------- - -			131--1-------- - -	
BRAMBLET Henry	11--1--------		BUCKNER Phil	-------------	
	11--1------- - -			------------- - 1	
BRAMBLET James	-22--1--1----		BUNTON John	1---1--------	
	2----1----- 1 -			----2------- - 2	
BRAMBLET Nathan	-122---1-----		BUNTON William	----22---1---	
	--1-1-1------ - -			--12---1----- - -	
BRAMBLETT Henry	--1---1------		BURCHFIELD Sarah	----1--------	
	--21-1------ - -			----11-1----- - -	
BRAMBLETT Ruth	1-------------		BURDIN Franklin	1---1--------	
	11---1-1----- 1 -			---1--------- - -	
BRAMBLETTE Henry	----2--------		BURDIN Garret	2-1--1-------	
	----1-------- - -			-3--1------- - -	
BRANCH Alvin	-111-1--------		BURDIN James	--1-1-1------	
	21--1--------- 4 -			111----------- - -	
BRANNUM William J	1----1-------		BURDIN Samuel	-1111-1------	
	1--1-------- - -			--12--1------- - -	
BREWER John H	2---1--------		BURNS Alvin	2---2--------	
	1--1-------- - -			1--11-------- 2 -	
BRIERLY Polly	-1-----------		BURNS Henry F	-1---1-------	
	-------1----- - -			11-11--------- - -	
BRIERLY Robert	-13-11--------		BURNS Matthew	21--1--2-----	
	2---1------- - -			-1-2-1------- - -	
BRIERLY Thomas	11-1---1-----		BURNS Robert	------1------	
	---1-1------- - -			------------- - -	
BRINEGAR Wiley	1-1--1--------		BURNS Samuel	-1111-1------	
	12---1------- - -			1121-1-------- - -	
BRINTON Samuel	--------1-----		BURNS Wesley	12--1--------	
	-------1--1---- - -			-1---1------ 4 -	
BRINTON William	11---1--------		BURNS William	2--12---1----	
	112--1-------- - -			11--1-1------- - -	
BROCK Tarlton	2111---1-----		BURRIS John	-11--1-------	
	--1---1------- - -			211--1-------- - -	
BROOKING Vivian	-1--1-11-----		BURRISS Alexander	12---1-------	
	---3-1-------- 1 -			2---1--------- 2 -	
BROOKS John	11--1---------		BUSBY Charles	--11-1-------	
	2---1--------- - -			--111-1------- - -	
BROOKS Mosely	211--1--------		BUSBY Rawley	1212--1------	
	11---1-------- - -			1111--1-------- - -	
BROOKS Zacheriah	----1---1----		BUZZARD Jacob	----1--------	
	---1---------- 5 -			-------1------ - -	
BROTHERS John	-111--1-------		BYERS John	-------1------	
	211--1-------- - -			-------1------ - -	
BROWN Archibald	-1211----1----		BYRAM Alfred	11---1-------	
	-1-2-1--1----- - -			-1-1---------- - -	
BROWN Daniel	12211--1----		BYRAM John	1---1--------	
	---11-1------- - -			----1--------- - -	
BROWN John	2----1--------		BYRAM Sarah	---2---------	
	----11-------- 1 -			--111-1----- - -	
BROWN Lanville	11-1--1------		BYRAN Wesley	------1------	
	12-1-1-------- 1 -			1---1--------- - -	
BROWN Matthew	2----1-------		Bowers Robert	---111-------	
	-------------- - -			111--1-------- 5 -	
BROWN Milton	111---1------		CALDWELL Anna	-1-----------	
	1122-1-------- - -			-1----1------- - -	
BROWN Samuel	2--1---------		CALDWELL David	----------1---	
	----1------- - -			---------1--- - -	
BRUNKER Samuel L	3-2--1--------		CALDWELL David A	-1---1-------	
	--1--1--1----- - -			-21--1-1----- - -	
BRYANT Daniel	-212--1-------		CALDWELL James	----1---1----	
	--2---1------- 1 -			--11---1------ 6 -	

Name	Census (row 1)	Census (row 2)
CALDWELL Robert	-1-------1-----	---11--1------ - -
CALL Daniel	----1---------	------------- 1 -
CALL Daniel	-------1-----	------1----- - -
CALL Daniel L	2---11-------	11--1----1--- - -
CALL John	1---1---------	----1--------- - -
CALL Samuel	13---1-------	--1--1-------- 3 -
CAMPBELL Ann *	-1--1---------	---2---1------ 1 -
CAMPBELL David	2------1------	-21--1-------- - -
CAMPBELL Elizabeth	--1-----------	------1-1----- - -
CAMPBELL Elizabeth	---11---------	-------1------ - -
CAMPBELL George	-121--1-------	-1-1---1------ - -
CAMPBELL Harrison	----1---------	1---1--------- - -
CAMPBELL Hugh	-111--1-------	-1----1------- 1 -
CAMPBELL James	----1---------	------1------- - -
CAMPBELL James	111-----1-----	121--1-------- - -
CAMPBELL John	21---1-------	11--1--------- - -
CAMPBELL John R	21---1-------	-111---------- 3 -
CAMPBELL Joseph	---2--1------	2-2-2-1------- - -
CAMPBELL Ogle	1211-1-------	11---1-------- - -
CAMPBELL Robert	--1-2----1---	---11--1------ 5 -
CAMPBELL Robert H	2---1---------	-1--1--------- 3 -
CAMPBELL William	1----1--------	----1--------- - -
CAMPBELL William	1-1-1-1-------	1222-1-------- - -
CAMPBELL Williamson	1312--1-------	--12--1------- - -
CAMROW Nancy	1111----------	---1--1------- - -
CARNAHAN Jackson	1----1--------	----1--------- - -
CARR George	1111--1-------	-121--1------- - -
CARTER George	------2-------	----1--------- 1 -
CARTER George L	-21--1-------	-1-1--1------- - -
CARTER John	--12-11-------	--1111-------- 7 -
CARTER Robert S	12--22-------	2----1-------- 4 -
CASE Melinda	1-111---------	-1111-1------- - -
CASEDAY James Jr	1-1--1-------	121-1--------- - -

Name	Census (row 1)	Census (row 2)
CASEDAY Robert	1---1---------	11--1-------- - -
CASIDAY James Jr	1-1-----1----	--1-1---1---- - -
CASIDAY Jeremiah	1-1--1-------	21---1------- - -
CASIDAY Joseph	----1--------	-1--1-------- - -
CASIDAY Robert T	------1------	-1--1-------- - -
CASITY Hiram	21--11-------	11---2------- - -
CAUGHEY James	---2--1------	1-23--------- - -
CHADWICK Ann	-1-1---------	-----1------- - -
CHAMBERS Abigail	-------------	-1-2--1------ 5 -
CHAMBERS Thomas	11--1-1------	111--1-------- - -
CHANEY Hillary	11--1--------	1---1--------- 3 -
CHAPPELL Edward F	--1---1-------	--1---1------- 3 -
CHARD James	-----1-------	21--1--------- - -
CHEATEM John	-21--1-------	1----1------- - -
CHERIS Henry T *	---------1---	----1-1------ 7 -
CHERIS John M *	1---3---------	---1--------- 2 -
CHILD Stanly F *	-----1-------	------------- - -
CHIPLEY John	31------1-----	-1-21--------- - -
CIDLE Thomas	121--1-------	-1---1------- - -
CLARK James	2---1---------	------------- - -
CLARK Jeremiah	---1---1-----	--------1----- 8 -
CLARK Nancy	---1-1-------	--------11--- 9 -
CLARK Thomas	11-21-1------	211----1----- - -
CLARK Thompson	-1-1-1-------	------1------ - -
CLAY James	11----1------	-11--1-------- 2 -
CLAY John	21---1-------	-2--1--------- 1 -
CLAYPOOLE John	2-1-1---------	-2--1---------
CLAYPOOLE Washington	3-2--1-------	-2--1---------
CLAYTON William	2-11---1-----	-1112---------
CLINKENBEARD John	122--1-------	2-1--1-------- - -
CLINKENBEARD Nancy	-------------	------1------ - -
COALMAN Hannah	-------------	----1--------- - -
COFFMAN Phillip	-112--1-------	--11-1------- 7 -

Name	Census
COLE John A	21-----1------ 111--1------- - -
COLIVER James	1-11--1------ 221--1------- - -
COLIVER John	-1--1-------- 21--1-------- - -
COLIVER Joseph	112---1------ -2-1-1------ 3 -
COLLIER Coleman A	-2------1---- -----1------- 8 -
COLLIER Elizabeth	----2-------- --1-11--1---- A -
COLLIER Elizabeth	------------- ---2---1------ G -
COLLINS Ambrose	1---1-------- ----1-----1--- - -
COLLINS Conway	----1-------- 1---1-------- - -
COLLINS Edmond Jr	1---1-------- ----1------- - -
COLLINS Edmond Sr	---1------1--- --1------1--- 6 -
COLLINS Thomas	---------1---- --111--1----- - -
COLLINS Thomas H	12---1-------- ---11-1------ 1 -
CONEY John	------------- ------------- - 4
CONN Martha	-11---------- -12---1------ 9 -
CONWAY Henry	-1111-------- ---2-1------ 7 -
CONWAY Nathaniel	-11---1------ 1-1--1---1--- 2 -
CONYERS Azariah	---1-1-------- -1--1--1----- - -
CONYERS Darius	----1-------- 2---1-------- 1 -
COOK Sarah	-2--1-------- ---2-1------- 9 -
COONS Elijah	212---1------ -1----------- 4 -
COONS Joseph	----1-------- ----1-------- 1 -
COOPER William B	2231--------- -1---1------ - -
CORD John	211--1------- 11---1------- - -
COSHOW John	-----------1--- -----------1--- - -
COTINGHAM William	-1-11-1------ 231--1------- - -
COTTINGHAM John	122--1------- 1--11-------- - -
COUCHMAN Andrew	1---21------- 21--1---1---- 6 1
COURTNEY George	1---1-------- -1-1--------- - -
COX Margaret	--1---------- --111--1----- - -
CRAIG John	-1---1------- 111-1-------- - -
CRAWFORD Alexander B	---21--1------ --112--1----- - -
CRAWFORD John	-1--1-------- 2----1------- - -
CRAY John R	----2-------- ------------- - 1
CRAY Martin L	---1---1---- --1---1------ - 1
CRAY Robert	-2---1------- 2-21-1------- - -
CRAYCRAFT Mary	-1-1-------- 1-2---1------ 1 -
CRAYCRAFT Thomas J	----11------- 1-1-1--2------
CRAYCRAFT Zaddock	1112--1------ 111-1-1------ - -
CRESS George	11--1-------- 1---1-------- 2 -
CROUCH Ambrose	1-21--1------ -21---1------ 1 -
CROUCH Ambrose D	2----1------- ----1------- - 1
CROUCH Baylis	1---1-------- -1--1--------
CROUCH David	----------1-- --------1-1--- -
CROUCH Harrison	----1-------- ----1--------
CROUCH John	------1--1--- ---------1--- 1 -
CROUCH Johnathan	--------1---- ----1-------
CRUMP Beverly	--1--1------- 221--1------- -
CRUMP Joseph	--1---1------ --1--1------- -
CRUMP Richard	212--1------- 1112-1--1---- -
CURTIS Jobe	11----1--1--- 111---1------ 6 -
CURTIS William Jr	1-1--1------- 1---1-------- - -
CURTIS William Sr	---------1--- -1-------1--- - -
DALE Franklin	------------- ------------- - 7
DALE Uriah	----11------- ----1-------- -
DALZELL Robert	31--1-1------ ---1-1------ 4 -
DAMPEER Henry	-2-1---1------ --1-1-1------ - -
DARNALL James	-1---1------- -1---1-------- - -
DARNELL James	----1-------- ----1-------
DARNELL Levi	--22---1----- ------1------
DAUGHERTY Benjamin	1----1------- ---1-1------- - -
DAVIDSON John *	---1--1------ -2-1-1------- 1 -
DAVIDSON Rachel	------------- ------------- - 1
DAVIDSON Thomas	----------1--- --------1---- - -
DAVIS James	1---1-------- -2--1-------- - -
DAVIS James	------------- ------------- - D

Name	Census	Name	Census
DAVIS Peter	------1-------- 1-----1-------- - -	DUNN William	---1----1---- ------1------ - -
DAY Leroy	1-----1-------- 11--1--------- - -	DUNNINGTON James	--1----1---- ----1--1---- - -
DAYTON William G	111---1-------- 1112-1-------- - -	DURRICKSON Jobe	------------- ------------- - B
DAZY Elijah	-------1----- --------1----- 9 -	DUTY John	-----1------- 111--1-------- 2 -
DAZY John	------------- ------------- - 1	DYER William	----------1--- ----------1--- - -
DAZY Mitchell	-------1----- ---1--------- 5 -	EADES Preston	1---1-------- ----1-------- 1 -
DEEN Abraham	-121-1-------- 11-----1------ - -	EALS John	21---1-------- -11-1--------- - -
DEEN Alexander	-11--1-------- 12-2-1-------- - -	EALS Washington	3-2-2--------- 1---1-1------- B -
DELAY Mary	---1---------- --111--1----- - -	EARLYWINE Daniel	1-12-1-------- 2211-1-------- - -
DELZELL Thomas	12---1-------- ----1----1--- 3 1	EARLYWINE Daniel	-1-2--1------ 11--1--------- - -
DENNY Thomas	----1-------- ----1-------- - -	EARLYWINE Jesse	1----1-------- 11--1--------- - -
DEWITT Jacob	-1111--1------ -212--1------ - -	EDWARDS Benjamin	-----2------- 1--1-1------ 2 -
DICKERSON Ann	------------- ------------- - 6	EDWARDS Benjamin	----1---1---- ----2--------- 1 1
DINSMORE Catherine	--1---------- ----2--1-1--- - -	EDWARDS John	---1---1------ ---11--1----- - -
DINSMORE Henry	--1-2--1------ -1-1--1------ - -	EDWARDS Robert L	211---1------ -22--1---1--- 2 -
DINSMORE Samuel	---1--1------- 121---1------ - -	ELLIOTT Ann	--13---------- -------1------ - -
DOLLAS William	--------1----- ------1--1---- - -	ELLIOTT Robert	----1---1---- ---1---1----- - -
DORRAL George	-------1-1---- ------------- - -	ELLIS Richard	1--11-------- 11---1-------- - -
DORRAL Henry O	1-----1-------- 1---1--------- 3 -	EVANS Gilead	---11-1------ -12---1-------
DOTSON Dudley	---------1----- ---------1----- - -	EVANS Joseph	12---1-------- 1-2--1-------- - -
DOTSON Elijah	--2-----1----- ----3--1------ - -	EVERMON Arthur	-211---1----- 1--21-1-------- - -
DOTSON Harrison	2----1-------- -1--1--1------ - -	EVERMON Samuel	1--1--------- --1---------- - -
DOTSON John	----1-------- ---1---------- - -	EWING George	11---1-------- 121-1--------- - -
DOTSON John	221--1-------- -1---1-------- - -	FARRAND Mark C	-11-1-------- 22--1--------- - -
DOTSON Martin	-1-1--1------ 1111--1------- - -	FEEBACK Amos	----1--------- --1-1--1------ - -
DOTSON Valentine	----1-------- 2---1--------- - -	FEEBACK Aris	----1--------- 22--1--------- - -
DOUGHARTY James	3------1------ -1---1-------- - -	FEEBACK Gilbert	-1211-1------ 121--1-------- - -
DOUGHERTY John *	---2--1------- ------1--------- 4 -	FEEBACK Jacob	-22-1-1------ ---12-1------ - -
DOUGHERTY John Jr	---1------1--- 2-2---1-------- - -	FEEBACK John	----1-------- ---1---------- - -
DOUGHERTY Thomas	2---1--------- 1---1--------- - -	FEEBACK John	-2111--1----- -1-11-1------- - -
DOUGHERTY Thomas	-------1----- 1-1--1-------- 8 -	FEEBACK Lewis	----1-------- 2---1--------- - -
DOUGHTY James	11---1-------- -11-1--------- - -	FIELD Abraham	--1-2--1----- --11---1----- - -
DOUGHTY William	----1---1----- --11--1------ - -	FIELDER Nancy	-1--1-------- ----1--------- 3 -

Name	Census marks
FIFER Catherine	----------1---- ------2--1---- - -
FISHBACK Charles	1----1------ 1---1--------- 1 -
FISHBACK Jane	----1------- --11---1------ 4 -
FISHBACK Josiah	-3----1------ 1---1--------- 1 -
FISHER Thomas	--12--1------ 1------1------ - -
FISHER William	----1------- ---1--------- 5 -
FITCHPATRICK James	------------1-- --1--11------- - -
FITCHPATRICK Jobe	11--1-------- ---------1---- - -
FITE Franklin	------1------- ---1--------- - -
FLETCHER Gilson	-11------1---- -------1------ - -
FLORA George	122--1-------- --1--1-------- - -
FLORA James	--1---1------ ---1---1--1-- - -
FLORA James	----1------- 1---1--------- - -
FLORA Madison	1---1-------- ---1--------- - -
FLORA Thomas	1---11------- -121-1-------- - -
FLORA William	------1------- 211--1-------- - -
FOOKS Stephen	-------------- -------------- - 2
FORGY John	1-1--1-------- 221-1--------- 1 -
FOSTER George	--2-11-------- ---1-1-------- 3 -
FOSTER Henry	--1------1--- --131--1------ 6 -
FOSTER James	----2-------- -------1------ - -
FOX Nathaniel	-1-11--1----- -1-1-1-------- 3 -
FRANKLIN Jefferson	21-11-------- -1---1-------- - -
FRITTS Henry *	----1-1------ -1-1--1------ 1 -
FRITTS William *	----1------- ----1--------- - -
FRYMAN Ann	-11--------- ------1------- - -
FRYMAN Jacob	2---1-1------ -221--1------- - -
FRYMAN Peter	----1------- 1---1--------- - -
FULLER Jesse	221-1-------- 2---1--------- - -
FULLER Joseph	-111----1---- ----1--------- - -
FULLER Nelson	----1-------- ----1--------- - -
FULTON Henry	1---1------ ----1--------- - -
FULTON John L	----1------- 2---1--------- - -
FULTON Samuel	1--11--1----- -111---1----- - -
GAFFIN Otho	-1--2--1----- ---21--1----- 1 -
GARDNER John	-1--1--1----- 2--1--1-----
GARDNER Samuel	---11 3321-1--------
GARRISON Alexander	-2-1-1------ -----1--------- - -
GARRISON Martin	----1--------- ---1--------- - -
GAY Joseph	---1--------- - - 21---1--------
GEOGHEGAN Milton	11--11-------- - - --11-1--------
GIFFORD Hiram	----1--------- 1 - 2-11-1--------
GILISPIE Alexander	1-21-1------- - - 111--1--------
GILLEN Jahue	11---------- 5 - 211---1--------
GITHENS John H	11-1-1------- - - 1-1--1--------
GLASCOCK Claybourn	-21-2-------- - - 111--1--------
GLENN Moses F	11---1-------- - - 132--1--------
GLENN Simeon	---2--1------- 1 - ---------1-----
GODARD Ignatious	---------1----- - - ---11
GONCE Benjamin	1---1--------- 5 - -1----1--------
GONCE George	--2--1--1----- - - -1--2-----1---
GONCE Martin	----2---1----- - - -121--1-------
GONCE Rachel	-11--1-------- - - ----1---------
GONCE Samuel	1--2-1--------- 2 - 2----1--------
GONCE Thomas	-----1--------- - - 2----1--------
GOODING Aron	121--1-------- - - ----1---------
GOODING Enoch	1---1--------- - - ---2---1------
GOODRICH Daniel	--1------1----- - - 2---1---------
GOODRICK John	1----11------- - - 13---1--------
GORE Benjamin	11---1-------- - - ----2-----1---
GOREM William	----1---1----- - - 12---1--------
GORMAN Daniel	2-1-1--------- 8 - --1------1----
GRAHAM Samuel	-----1--------- - - ---1---------1-
GRAVES Margaret	--------1------ - - --------------
GRAVES William B	11-1-1-------- 2 - -1--1-1-------
GRAY Andrew	12--1--1------ - - 11---1-------- -1--1---------- - -

Name	Tally
GRAY Andrew F	12----1-------
	1--1-1-------- - -
GRAY Catherine	----1---------
	----2--1----- - -
GRAY Elijah	22---1--------
	--1--1------- - -
GRAY Harrison	----1---------
	2---1-------- - -
GRAY James	----1--1------
	---1----1---- - -
GRAY Joseph	2---1---------
	----1-------- - -
GRAY Samuel	22--1---------
	1-1-1-------- - -
GRAY Squire	11---1--------
	-1-1--------- - -
GRAY Thomas	2---1---------
	1-1-1-------- - -
GRAY William	1---2---------
	111-1-------- - -
GRAY William F	-1111--1------
	-11---1------ - -
GRIFFITH William	-1---1--------
	22--1--------- 2 -
GRIGG William	----211-------
	112--1------- - -
GRIGSBY Frances	------1-------
	------1------ 2 -
GROSS Henry	2---1---------
	1----1------- - -
HABER Thomas	-1-22-1-------
	--3---1------ 2 -
HALE Preston	-----1--------
	1----1------- 4 -
HALL Abraham	-1--1---------
	---1--------- - -
HALL Isaac	1---1---------
	-2-1--------- - -
HALL John	--1--1--------
	33--11--1---- 7 -
HALL John	1----1--------
	-2-1--------- 3 -
HALL Moses	--1---1-------
	--------1---- 3 -
HALL Robert C	---1---1------
	-22---1------ 7 -
HALL Viney	-------------
	------------- - 2
HALL William	--------1-----
	--------1---- 4 -
HAM Burton R *	2---1---------
	----1-------- 2 -
HAM Caleb L	1---1---------
	2---1-------- - -
HAM Elizabeth	----1---------
	----11--1---- - -
HAM Elizabeth	--22----------
	----1-1------ - -
HAM Jacob M	1---1---------
	1--1--------- - -
HAM John	---211-1------
	--1-----1---- 2 -
HAM John Jr	-----1---1----
	----2-------- - -
HAM Michael	-11-111-------
	11-2--1------ - -
HAM Samuel	21---1--------
	--2-1-------- - -
HAM Thomas	-11-1---------
	1--1-1------- - -
HAM Thomas	-1--1---------
	11--1-------- - -
HAMILTON Elenor	--21----------
	-1-1--1------ - -
HAMILTON Jane	----31--------
	--112--1----- - -
HAMILTON John	2---1---------
	--121--------
HAMILTON John	-1111-1-------
	311---1------ 2 -
HAMILTON William	---22-1-------
	--11---1----- 1 -
HAMM William	-------1------
	------------- - -
HARBER David	1---1---------
	11--1-------- - -
HARBER Joshua	----1---------
	1---1-------- - -
HARBET John	1112---1------
	-1121-1------ - -
HARBET Philip G	1---1---------
	----1-------- - -
HARDIN Robert W	21--11--------
	12--1-------- 1 -
HARDMAN Jacob	--1------1----
	----1-------- 1 -
HARDWICK Henry	----2--1------
	-1-2--1------ - -
HARDWICK Jesse	----1---------
	----1-------- - -
HARDWICK John	-----1--------
	1--1-1-------- - -
HARNEY Ann	12------------
	--22-1------- - -
HARNEY Elijah	-12--1--------
	1--1-1-------- - -
HARNEY Gilbert	2---1---------
	1---1--------- - -
HARNEY Willoby	2---1---------
	1---1-------- - -
HARRIS George	---211--------
	1------1------ - -
HARRIS John	--11---1------
	---1---1------ - -
HARRIS Sophia	-------------
	---1--1------ - -
HARRIS William	1---1---------
	2---1-------- - -
HARRISON John R	13---1--------
	-----1-------- - -
HARRISON William	22---1--------
	-----1-------- - -
HARTLEY William	1--2--1-------
	--21--1------ - -
HAVENS George	-11----1------
	---1--1------ - -
HAWKINS Samuel	---1----------
	1--1--------- - -
HAWKINS Squire	1---1---------
	11--1-------- - -
HAWKINS Valentine	-12--1--------
	--1--1------- - -

```
HAWKS Charles        22-1--1-------
                     1121-1--------- - -
HEADRECK William     2----1--------
                     1----1-------- 1 -
HEADRICK Michael     --1---1-------
                     ---111-------- - -
HEDING Solomon       ----1---1----
                     ----11---1---- - -
HEDRICK John         --1-1---------
                     ------1-------- - -
HENDERSON Benjamin   --------------
                     -------------- - 5
HENDRIX Isaac        -------1-------
                     221--1--------- - -
HENDRIX James        1---1---------
                     -----1-------- - -
HENDRIX John         1-111--1-----
                     1-112--1----- - -
HENDRIX Peter        1-----1-------
                     -----1-------- - -
HENDRIX Rebeckah     --11---------
                     --1--1--------- - -
HENRY Richard D *    -11--1-1-----
                     ----------1---- - -
HENSEY John          1-11--1-------
                     -121-1--------- - -
HENSON George        -2-3---1-----
                     31----1--------- - -
HENSON Thomas        1---1---------
                     ----1--------- - -
HERNDON Elizabeth    -2------------
                     -13-1---1---- 1 -
HERNDON Thomas C     ----1---1-----
                     ----------1--- - -
HERNTON Washington   -----1--------
                     ----1--------- - -
HIAT Elizabeth       --1-1--1------
                     ---1---1------ 8 -
HIATT Henry          ---1---------
                     ----1--------- - -
HIGGINS William      1---111-------
                     1---2--------- 1 -
HIGHLANDER George    1-12------1---
                     111-1-1-------- - -
HILDRETH Aquila      -2--1---------
                     ----2---1---- - -
HILDRETH John        11--1-1-------
                     ---1--1------ 4 -
HILDRETH John        ------1-------
                     3---1--------- - -
HILDRETH William     21---1--------
                     1111-1--1---- - -
HILL Moses           1---1---------
                     1---1--------- - -
HILL Otho            -1-12-1-------
                     1-11--1-------
HILLOCK James        -11-2---1----
                     --11---1----- 1 -
HILLOCK John         ----1---------
                     1---1--------- - -
HILLOCK William      ----1---------
                     12--1--------- - -
HIND John W          1---1---1----
                     --------1---- 3 -
HIND Thomas H        1-1--1--------
                     -11--1------- 5 -

HOLLADAY John        -11---1------
                     1--1--1------ B -
HOLLADAY Thomas      --1-2-1------
                     11-11-------- A -
HOLLADAY William     -11--1--------
                     21---1------- B -
HOLLER Franklin      1------1------
                     2----1-------- - -
HOLLER John          1---1--1------
                     1--1--1------- 1
HOLLER Joseph        1121-1--------
                     11---1--------- - -
HOLLER Mary          ---1----------
                     ---------1----- - -
HOOK William         --3--11------
                     1---1--------- - -
HOPKINS Elizabeth    --------------
                     -------1------ - -
HOPKINS John         11-1-1--------
                     11---1-------- - -
HOPKINS Joslin       1-212-1-------
                     -2----1----- 6 -
HOPKINS Moses        -------1-------
                     -------------- 8 -
HORNBACK Adam        ---------1----
                     1---2--1----- 7 -
HORNBACK John        ---------1----
                     -1-21-1------ 1 -
HORNBACK John        -----1--------
                     ----1-------- 3 -
HORNBACK Peter       2---1---------
                     --111-1------ - -
HOSSMAN James        2----1--------
                     -1---1-------- 4 -
HOUSE John           2---1---------
                     1------1------ - -
HOW Andrew E         ----1---------
                     ----1--------- - -
HOW Anna             ---21---------
                     --1-1--1---1- - -
HOW Peter            --111-1-------
                     -111---1------ - -
HOWARD Alexander     1---1---------
                     1---1--------- - -
HOWARD Daniel        1---1---------
                     1---1-------- 5 -
HOWARD Joel *        11-111--------
                     -11-1-1------ 1 -
HOWE Anna            --1-1---------
                     -1----1------ 2 -
HOWE Dunlap          -2--11--------
                     1---1--------- 3 -
HOWES Elizabeth      ----1---------
                     --12--1------ - -
HOWES John           ----1---------
                     1---1--------- - -
HOWES Reuben         -3222--1-----
                     -1-1-1-------- - -
HUBANKS Wesley       1----1--------
                     1---1--------- - -
HUBANKS William      -1-21-1-------
                     1111--1------- - -
HUBBLE Harvey        ----1---------
                     1---1--------- - -
HUDDLESTON David     21-1--1-------
                     12--2--------- - -
```

HUFFMAN Henry S	-------1------ --1--1------ - -	JOHNSON Laban	-----1------- 1---1------- 4 -
HUFFMAN John R	-------1----- ------1------ - 9	JOHNSTON Johnathan	---1--1----- -------1----- 6 -
HUFFSTUTTER John	--111---1---- ------1------ 4 -	JOHNSTON William	---1--1----- -------1----- - -
HUGHES Claybourn	1---1-------- ----1------ - -	JOLLY James	-11--1------ 122--1------ - -
HUGHES George	1211-1------ 12--2-------- - -	JONES Drury	---------1--- 1---1--1----- - -
HUGHES Grayson	11---1------ 232--1-1----- - -	JONES Jacob	------------- ------------- - 5
HUGHES Isaac	---1--1----- ------1------ 1 -	JONES John	------1------ ------------- 8 -
HUGHES John	12---1------ 1---1--------- - -	JONES Lewis	----1--1---- --11--1------ - -
HUGHES John	------------- ------------- - 8	JONES William R	--------1---- ------------- 8 -
HUGHES John *	21-21-1------ 2-1--1------- 1 -	JOURDON Samuel	------------- ------------- - 3
HUGHES Pratt	------1----- ----1-1------ - -	KEITH John	------1------ ------------- - -
HUGHES Robert *	1----1------ ----1------ 1 -	KENADAY David	--1-1-------- -1--1------ - -
HULL David	221--1------ 111---1----- - -	KENADAY John	21--1-------- 1---1------ - -
HULL William	11--1-------- ----1-------- - -	KENADAY Robert	--------1---- --------1--- - -
HUTCHINS Cader	2-2----1----- ---1--1------ D -	KENEDAY Claybourn	2----1------ -1--1------ - -
HUTCHINSON Rebeckah	------------- ------1------ - -	KENNY James	------------- -----1------ - -
HUTSELL Jacob	1--11--1----- --11---1----- - -	KENNY John C	11--1-------- --1--1------ - -
ISHEOM Unice	-1----------- 1----1----1-- 1 -	KENNY Madison	--1--1------- -----1------ - 1
ISHMAEL Benjamin	12---1------- 1---1--------- - -	KENNY Willis	--11-------- -----1------ - -
ISHMAEL Samuel	21--1-------- --321-1------ - -	KENTON William	12--1-------- -1221-1------ - -
JACKSON James	1---1-------- 21--1--------- - -	KERN Levi	12-21-1------ 1---1------ 3 -
JACKSON John	11111-1------ 121--1------- - -	KERN Simeon	1---1-------- --------1---- - -
JACKSON John	1---1-------- 11-11-------- - -	KERN Thomas	--------1---- -11-1--1----- - -
JACKSON Tamer	------------- ------------- - 6	KERNS Levi	--111-1------ ------------- - -
JEWEL Allen	-2-1----1---- --2-2--1------ - -	KERNS Viney	------------- ------------- - 3
JEWEL Wesley	2---1-------- ----1------ - -	KIMBROUGH John	------------- ----1------- - 1
JEWEL William	1---1-------- 1---1-------- - -	KIMBROUGH Samuel	----1-------- 1---1-1------ 4 -
JIMESON Franklin	1---1-------- ----1-------- - -	KIMES Elizabeth	---11------- 1---1------ 2 -
JOHNSON Benjamin F	--1---------- ----2-------- - -	KIMES Peter	------------- ---11---1---- - -
JOHNSON Greenberry	-------1---- 3 - ------------- - 2	KIMES Stephen	---11---1---- 1-1---1------ - -
JOHNSON James	1---1-------- ----2-------- 1 -	KIMES William	22---1------- 21--11------- - -
JOHNSON James H	----1-------- 1--1--------- 3 -	KIMES William	-1--1------- 111---1------ 1 -
JOHNSON John T	----1-------- 2---1------ - -	KINCAID Samuel B	111111-------- -1---1------ 11--1-------- - -

```
KINCAID William C      -----1---------
                       ---1---------- 3 -
KINCAID Willis         -----1---------
                       ----11-1----- - -
KINCART John           11-2--1------
                       -21---------- - -
KING Sabina            --2----------
                       -111--1------ - -
KNOX David             21---1-------
                       1----1-------
KOOKENDOFFER Christian 1121-1-------
                       ---11-1----- - -
LAMAR Nathan           111--1-------
                       -2--1-------- - -
LAWRENCE Harrison      1---1--------
                       ---1-------- - -
LAWRENCE James         1--11--------
                       2---1------- - -
LAWRENCE John          1---1--------
                       1--1-------- - -
LAWRENCE Lewis         21---1-------
                       -1--1------- - -
LAWRENCE William       11211-1------
                       111---1------ - -
LAYTHAM Barbary        1------------
                       -1---1-------- 2 -
LEACH Tabitha          --1-2--------
                       ---2--1------ - -
LEDFORD William        3---1--------
                       -1--1--------- 4 -
LILLY Nancy            ---1---------
                       --1----1----- - -
LINN Alexander         1-3-1----1---
                       11121-1------ - -
LINN Timothy           ---1---1------
                       -1--11------ - -
LINVILL Wilford        ----1--------
                       1---1------- - -
LINVILLE Aron          11--1--------
                       3---1------- - -
LINVILLE Jacob B       111----------
                       121--1------ - -
LINVILLE John          ---1----1----
                       --1-1--1----- - -
LINVILLE Lewis         --11---1-----
                       -1111--1----- - -
LITTON John H          1--1-1-------
                       -1--1------- - -
LITTON William W       -1---1-------
                       2----1------- 1 -
LIVENGOOD Philip       ---1--1------
                       ---2--1------ - -
LOCKRIDGE Catherine    -------------
                       --122--1----- - -
LOGAN Michael          3--22-1------
                       --21--1------ - -
LONG Eliaken           --11---1-----
                       ---------1---- 6 -
LONG John              ------2------
                       1----1------- 2 -
LOUDERBACK Isaac       --1----1-------
                       211--1-1----- - -
LOW Isaac              11--1--------
                       -11--1------- - -
LOW Samuel             11--1--------
                       2----1------- - -

LOWE Squire            12---1-------
                       2-1--1------- - -
LUCKEY James           11---1-------
                       -----1------- 5 -
LYONS William          ----1--------
                       1---1------- - -
MABERRY John           -------------
                       ------------- - 7
MACKLEY William        -1-3---1-----
                       -12--1------- 3 -
MADDEN Isaac           ------1------
                       -------1----- - -
MADDOX Bennet          1--------1---
                       111-1--1----- - -
MADDOX Henry           -----1-------
                       ---1--------- - -
MAFFET Matthew         11--1--------
                       1---1------- - -
MAFFET William         -----1-------
                       21---2------- - -
MAHUGH Anna            -------1-----
                       ---1--1------ 1 -
MAHUGH Laban D         2111---1-----
                       --21-1------- - -
MAINER Stephen         1-------1----
                       -1--1---1---- - -
MAIRS Andrew           21---1-------
                       --1--1------- - -
MALORY George          -------------
                       ------------- - 2
MAN jacob              211--1-------
                       1-1--1------- - -
MANGUS Jacob           -1---1-------
                       111--1-1----- - -
MANN Amos              2---1--------
                       12--1-------- - -
MANN Charles           1----1-------
                       21---1------- - -
MANN David             12---1-------
                       1---1-------- - -
MANN David             1---1--------
                       1---1-------- - -
MANN James             ---11--------
                       ---1--------- - -
MANN John Jr           -1---1-------
                       211-1-------- - -
MANN John Sr           --1-----1----
                       12-1-1--1---- - -
MANN Peter             ----1---2----
                       ----1---1---- - -
MANN Samuel            3---1--------
                       ----1-------- - -
MANN William           1----1-------
                       -2---1------- - -
MANNIX John            ----2---1----
                       ---12-------- - -
MARCHET John           1---21-------
                       --1--1------- - -
MARSH Abraham          -------1-----
                       --1----1----- - -
MARSHALL Samuel        ----1--------
                       1----1------- - -
MARSHALL Silas         ----1--------
                       ----1-------- - -
MARSTON Lyford *       ----1--------
                       1---1------- - -
```

MARTIN Edmund	--212--1-----	MITCHELTREE John	--------1-----
	-211---1------ 9 -		--1----1------ - -
MARTIN John	-1---1--------	MOLER Elizabeth	--1-3---------
	1--11--1------ - -		---21--1------ - -
MARTIN Nehemiah	121----1------	MOLER Isaac	---2----1-----
	1-1--1-------- - -		--111-1------- - -
MARTIN Thomas	21-1-1--------	MOLER John	-----1--------
	122--1-------- - -		-1--1---1----- - -
MASSIE William	-1-11---------	MOLER John	21--11--------
	2-----1------ - -		-1-1-1-------- - -
MASTIN Caleb	111---1-------	MOORE Anna	-------------
	-121--1------ - -		-1--1--------- - -
MATCHET James *	----11--------	MOORE Aron	----1---------
	2--1--------- - -		2--1--------- - -
MATEER William	-------1------	MOORE John A	--1---1-------
	------------- - -		---21-1------- - -
MATHERS Alexander	----1---------	MOORE Stanley	----11--------
	2--1---------- - -		----1--1----- - 1
MATHERS Barton W	-12--1--------	MOORE Thomas	-112----1-----
	--1-1--------- 1 -		---2---1------ - -
MATHERS Gavin	-------1------	MOORE William	3---1---------
	--12--1------- 1 -		----1-------- - -
MATHERS James	--3-1-1-------	MOORE Zedekiah	---12--1------
	11-----1------ - -		---2--1------- 3 -
MATHERS Polly	---1----------	MORGAN John J	------1-------
	--21--1------- 1 -		------------- - -
MATHERS Robert M	2-----1-------	MORGAN John S	211-1-1-------
	11--1--------- - -		11--2--------- C 1
MATHERS Sarah	--1-----------	MORGAN William F	----1---------
	-------1------ - -		1---1-------- 2 -
MATHERS Thomas	1-1---1-------	MORRIS Daniel	--2-1--1------
	1111-1-------- - -		11----1------ 4 -
MATHERS William	1-1----1------	MORRIS Thomas	1-11--1-------
	1--1---1----- 3 -		11-1-1-------- - -
MEDLIN Richard	121---1-------	MOSS James	1---1---------
	2-2--1-------- - -		11--1--------- - -
MEEKS James	-2---1--------	MOULDEN Reason	-1--1---------
	-32--1-------- - -		21--1--------- - -
MEEKS John	-1--2-1-------	MUFFORD Nelly	-------------
	1112--1------- - -		------------- - 2
MENACH J Ant	-11----1------	MULICAN Archibald	1-2----1------
	2-122-1------- - -		---111-1------ - -
MENEFEE Jonas	-1-1--1-------	MULICAN Benjamin	2---11--------
	----1-------- 5 -		1-1-1--------- - -
MERIMEE Richard	11---1--------	MULICAN Francis	1---1---------
	2---1--------- - -		----1-------- - 1
METCALFE Melville *	3-----1-------	MULICAN Samuel	----1---------
	----1--------- 4 -		-1------------ - -
METCALFE Thomas	----2---1-----	MULICAN Sarah	1-------------
	--21---1------ D -		-1---1-------- - -
MILLER James	--1-1--1------	MULICAN William	1----1--------
	-1111--1------ - -		1----1------- 1 -
MILLER John	121---1-------	MURPHY George W	---21---1-----
	11---1-------- - -		---1---------- - -
MILLER John	----1---------	MURPHY William	1----1--------
	-1---1-------- - -		3----1-------- - -
MILLER John	--1-1---1-----	MURRAY John	----1---------
	---1----1----- 6 -		1---1-1------- - -
MILLER Robert	-------1------	MYERS Abraham	11111--1------
	------1------- 1 -		1-21-1-------- - -
MILLER William	111--1--------	MYERS Adam	-1111--1------
	1-1--1-------- 4 -		---11--1------ - -
MILTELL Silas	-1-1--1-------	MYERS Benjamin	2-111-1-------
	---111-------- 7 -		----1------1-- - -
MITCHELL William	1-11--1-------	MYERS George	21211--1------
	-221--1------- - -		-21--1-------- - -

```
MYERS Henry             ----1---1-----        McFARLAND Jesse         ----1---------
                        1----2-1------- - -                           ----1--------- - -
MYERS Henry V           111--1--------        McFARLAND Margaret      11-1----------
                        11---1-------- 2 -                            --1-1---1---- - -
MYERS Jacob             -1---1--------        McGINNIS Elizabeth      ----2---------
                        1--11---1---- - -                             --12--1------ - -
MYERS James             2---1--------         McGINNIS Levi           1--2----------
                        ----1-------- - -                             ---11-------- 2 -
MYERS William           ----1--------         McILVAIN Andrew         11---1--------
                        ----1-------- - -                             --2---1------- 5 -
MYERS William           ------1--------        McINTIRE David          -11--1--------
                        -1-11-------- - -                             121--1-------- - -
McANALT Prudence        -------------         McINTIRE James          1---1---------
                        1----1--1---- - -                             2---1-------- - -
McCABE William          ------1--------        McINTIRE John           --1-1--1------
                        --1----------- - -                            -111---1------ 1 -
McCALL William          -2---11-------        McMAHAN Daniel          ----2---------
                        -11--1-------- - -                            --1----------- 1 -
McCLANAHAN Charles      1--1--1-------        McMAHAN John *          -1-1-1--------
                        1-2-2---1---- - -                             1-2--1------- 1 -
McCLANAHAN John         11----1-------        McMAHAN Robert          ----11--------
                        -2---1-------- - -                            221--1-------- - -
McCLARY Robert          1----1--------        McMAHAN William         1---2---------
                        -21---1------- - -                            2---1--1----- - -
McCLINTOCK Alexander    -1--11--------        McMILLAN John F *        ----2---------
                        ---1-1--1--- 1 -                              ----2-------- 1 -
McCLINTOCK Hugh         ----11--1-1--         McMILLEN Samuel         -1-1-1--------
                        ------------- 1 -                             1---1-------- 3 -
McCLINTOCK Nancy        1--1--1-------        McQUOWN Ephraim         1-131---------
                        ---1-1------- 1 -                             ----1-------- - -
McCLURE Peter H         ----1---------        McQUOWN Lawrence        121---1-------
                        ----1-------- - -                             --2--1-------- - -
McCONNAUGHHAY John      ----------1---        McQUOWN William         ------1--------
                        12--12-------- - -                            1---1-------- - -
McCONNAUGHHAY John Jr   12---1--------        McVEY John              21-1---1------
                        -1---1-------- - -                            -111--1------- - -
McCORD John             --111-1-------        McVEY John C            2---1---------
                        ---1---1------ - -                            ----1-------- - -
McCORMACK Thomas J      1231-1--------        McVEY Perrin            1---1---------
                        112--1-------- 5 -                            11--1-------- - -
McCULLOUGH Franklin     1---1---------        McVEY William H         ----1---------
                        1---1-------- - -                             ----1-------- - -
McCUNE Elijah           1-1---1-------        NEAL Henry              2---1---------
                        1----1---1--- - -                             -----1------- - -
McCUNE Jesse            12---1--------        NEAL John               --121--1------
                        1-1--1-------- - -                            -1--1--------- E -
McCUNE John             21-1-1--------        NEAL William            11----1-------
                        -211-1-------- - -                            2---11-------- 2 -
McCUNE Robert           1-----1-------        NEAL Winston            121---1-------
                        1----1-------- - -                             -11--1-------- - -
McCUNE Robert Jr        1-111--1------        NICHOLS Henry           ----1---------
                        ----1--1----- - 1                             ---1-------- 1 -
McCUNE Samuel           ------1--------        NOBLE Charles           ---1--1--------
                        -------------- - -                            ------2-------- - -
McDONALD George         1---1---------        NORTON Hiram            121-1-1-------
                        12--1--1----- - -                             1121-1-------- B -
McDONALD Hugh           ----3--1------        NORVILLE William *      -----1--------
                        ---1--1------ - -                             1--1-------- 2 -
McDONALD Jane           --1-----------        NUN Jacob               --------------
                        -1--1--1---- - -                              -------------- - 2
McDONALD Nimrod         23---1--------        O´NEAL Nancy *          --1-----------
                        -----1--1---- - -                             1-1--1-------- - -
McDOWELL John           ----1---------        OCHERMAN John           1---1---------
                        ----1-------- - -                             ---1-------- 5 -
McDOWELL Robert         1-----2-------        ODEN Volney B           11---1--------
                        132--1----1-- - -                             1---1-------- - -
```

Name	Census data
ODEN William C	12--1-1--------
	11--1--------- 2 -
OGDEN Enos	-111---1-----
	---1-1------- - -
OGDEN James	----1--------
	----1-------- - -
OGDEN Lucy *	-------------
	--1---1----- 3 -
ONEAL Nancy	---1---------
	--11---1----- - -
ORR John	--111--1-----
	---1--1----11 5 -
OVERBAY Henry H	2---1--------
	-----1------- 2 -
OVERBAY John	1----1-------
	-1---11------ 2 -
OVERBAY Richard M	1---1--------
	----1------- 2 -
OVERBY Samuel B	----1-------
	2---1-------- - -
OWINGS John	--------1-----
	--112-1------- - -
OWINGS Joshua	------1------
	----1-------- - -
PAINTER Ezra	11-11---------
	1---1-------- - -
PARISH Johnathan	-11---1------
	--1---1------ 1 -
PARKER Charles	--2-11--1----
	-112---1----- 6 -
PARKER George	----1-------
	11--1-------- - -
PARKER John	1----1-------
	1---1-------- 3 -
PARKER Robert	-11--1-------
	2---1-------- 2 -
PARKER Solomon	1-131--1-----
	-21---1------ - -
PARKER William	-----1-------
	21--1---1---- - -
PARKS Arthur L	1---111------
	11--1-------- 1 -
PARKS John G *	---1---1-----
	--1---1------ 3 -
PARKS Joseph	211---1------
	------------- 1 -
PARKS Thomas	-----11------
	1---1-------- 2 -
PASLEY John	----1-------
	1---1-------- - -
PASLEY Mary	--1---------
	-1-21-1------ - -
PATTON John	--1-11-------
	-2-1-1------- 5 -
PATTON Samuel	21---1--------
	12--1-------- - -
PAXTON Robert	--1-1---1----
	-------11---- - -
PAXTON Singleton	11---1-------
	----1-------- - -
PAYNE Berry	----1--1-----
	----1--1----- - -
PAYNE James	----1--------
	----1------- - -
PAYNE William	----1--------
	1---1-------- 4 1
PAYNE William	11--1---------
	2---1--------- - -
PAYTON Rachel	-------------
	------------- - 8
PEOPLES Matilda	-------------
	------1----- - -
PETERSON Henry	-122--1-----
	211--1-1----- - -
PHILIPS James	1---1--------
	2---1-------- - -
PHILIPS John	111---1-----
	111121------- - -
PIPER Isreal *	-1--1--------
	21--1-------- 2 -
PIPER James R	--1--1--1----
	----1--1----- 7 -
PIPER John F	111---1------
	1---1-------- 4 1
PIPER John P *	111--1-------
	21--1-------- - 1
PIPER Robert	----21-1-----
	---1--1----- - -
PIPER Samuel C	-21--1-------
	1-1-1-------- 5 -
POICEL James	1----1-------
	----1-------- 2 -
POISEL Matilda	-------------
	-1--1-1----- - -
POLLOCK James	1-112--------
	1---1-------- 8 -
PORTER Henry	---1--------
	-----1------- - -
PORTER Robert	----1-------
	1---1-------- -
POTTS Henry	2112--11-----
	-1--1-------- - -
POTTS James	1-1--21------
	1211-1-------- 6 -
POTTS John	1--1----1----
	-1-111-1----- - -
POTTS William	1-1--1-------
	12--1-------- 1 -
POWEL Charles	---1----1----
	-------1----- - -
POWEL Nathan	-1-1--1------
	2----1------- 1 -
POWEL William	21---1-------
	-1--1-------- - -
POYNTER Johnathan	-------1-----
	-------1----- - -
POYNTER William	11--1---------
	---1-------- - -
PRATHER Barruch	----31--1----
	---1----1---- 7 -
PRATHER Benjamin	1---1--------
	1---1-------- - -
PRATHER Benjamin	121---1------
	1-1--1-------- - -
PRATHER Benjamin Jr	-2-11--1-----
	---1--1----- 6 -
PRATHER Benjamin W	----1-------
	1--1-------- 5 -
PRICE Joseph	3111--1------
	-12--1------- - -
PRYOR Catherine	----211------
	----211------ 4 -

PULLY George	`---------------`	`-------------- - 4`
PURCELL Elijah	`----1--1-----`	`1--11--1----- - -`
PURCELL John	`----1--------`	`1---1-------- - -`
PURCELL William	`11--1--------`	`1---1-------- - -`
QUIETT Greenup	`1---1--------`	`1---1-------- - -`
QUIETT James	`--------1-----`	`--------1----- - 1`
RAMSEY Levi	`--------------`	`-------------- - 8`
RANKIN Elizabeth	`-111---------`	`----1-1------ - -`
RANKIN John	`211--1-------`	`--1--1------ - -`
RANKIN John S	`----1--------`	`1---1-------- - -`
RATLIFF Coalman	`---11`	`11--1-1------ - -`
RAYMON John M	`1-11-1-------`	`12-1-1------- - -`
REEDE Crawford	`---1---------`	`------------- - -`
REEDE James	`111--1-------`	`11-2-1------- - -`
REID Jacob	`---12--1-----`	`--11---1----- - -`
REVEAL James	`--------1-----`	`------------- - -`
REVEAL Joseph Jr	`1----1-------`	`---1--------- - -`
REVEAL Joseph Sr	`-1------1----`	`--------1---- 2 -`
RIBELAND Catherine	`-------------`	`--------1---- 1 -`
RICE George	`---11--------`	`2---1-------- 1 -`
RICHALS William	`2----1-------`	`122--1------- - -`
RICHARDSON James	`---------1---`	`--------1--- - -`
RICHARDSON Polly	`1-211--------`	`--1-1------- - -`
RICHESON Greenberry	`1---1--------`	`2---1-------- - -`
RIDDLE Peter	`-------------`	`------------- 1 3`
RIDDLE William	`--------1----`	`-------11---- 5 -`
RIDGELO John	`--2----1-----`	`1--1---1----- - -`
RIELY Nancy	`1-111--------`	`---1--1----- - -`
RIGG Clement	`----1---2----`	`--12--1------ - -`
RIGG Nancy	`22-----------`	`-----1------ - -`
RIGGS Erasmus	`----2---1----`	`---112--1---- F -`
RILEY John	`12-1-1-------`	`111-1-------- 1 -`
RITCHEY Catherine	`12-----------`	`--1--1------- - -`
RITCHEY Esau	`--1-1---1----`	`--------1----- - -`
RITCHEY Gilbert	`----1--------`	`----1-------- - -`
RITCHEY Henry	`----1--------`	`1--1-------- - -`
RITCHEY Henry	`--1-1-1------`	`--12---1----- - -`
RITCHEY Isaac	`------1---1---`	`----1-----1--- - -`
RITCHEY Jesse	`1---1--------`	`22--1-------- - -`
RITCHEY Mason	`12--1--------`	`-1--2-------- - -`
RITCHEY Minor	`--1-1--------`	`--------1----- - -`
RITCHEY Solomon	`11--1--------`	`11--1-------- - -`
RITCHEY Thomas	`----1--------`	`1--1---------- 1 -`
RITCHEY Wilford N	`--1-1--------`	`1--1-------- - -`
RITCHEY William	`11-2--1-------`	`1121-1-------- - -`
RITCHEY Zacheus	`3-111-1-------`	`12-2--1------- - -`
ROBERTS Eli	`1-1--1--------`	`11--1-------- - -`
ROBERTS Henley	`-1-1-1-1------`	`--11--1------- - -`
ROBERTS Lewis	`1---1--------`	`----1-------- - -`
ROBERTSON John M	`--2-1---1----`	`---1---1------ 2 -`
ROBINSON James *	`-1---1--------`	`2---1-------- - -`
ROBINSON John	`2----11-------`	`-2----1------- - -`
ROBINSON John F *	`----1--------`	`---1-------- - -`
ROBY Levin	`21---1--------`	`-1--1-------- - -`
ROBY Napoleon	`1---1--------`	`11--1-------- - -`
ROGERS Henry	`1---1--------`	`1---2-------- - -`
ROGERS Henry	`-------------`	`-------------- - 7`
ROGERS James	`122---1-------`	`1--1--1------- - -`
ROGERS John	`-----1--------`	`-----1-------- - -`
ROGERS John	`---1--1-------`	`-1-2-1-------- - -`
ROGERS Thomas J	`------1-------`	`-------------- - -`
ROGERS Willis	`212--1--------`	`--2--1-------- 2 -`
ROLL Nathaniel	`2---1--------`	`12---1-------- 2 -`
ROSS Greenberry *	`--3---1-------`	`11---1-------- 1 -`
ROSS Tilman	`----1--1------`	`-----1-1------ - -`
ROSS William	`-1---1--------`	`11--1-------- - -`

Name	Census marks
ROSSER Mahala	11------------
	-1---1--------- 1 -
ROUNDTREE Newton	-21---1-------
	1-1--1--------- - -
ROYSE Alphred	----1----------
	------------- - -
ROYSE Morgan	----1----------
	---1---------- - -
ROYSE Solomon	11-----1-------
	11-1-1--------- 5 -
RUDDLE George	--1-1--1------
	-1-1--1------- 7 -
RUNNELS Mary	-----1--------
	-------1------ 1 -
RUSSELL Fenton	-2-----1------
	2-21-1--------- - -
RUTH John P	1----1--------
	-2--1--------- - -
SADLER Burrel *	--1-1---------
	-------------- - -
SADLER Edward	2---1--1------
	----1---1----- - -
SADLER Jesse	1-1--1--------
	-11-1---------- - -
SALMONS John	1--2---1------
	-21-1---------- - -
SAMPSON Abraham	-111-1--------
	12---1--------- - -
SANDERS James	----------1--
	----------1--- - -
SANDERS John	12-2-1--------
	--31-1--------- - -
SCOBEE Stephen	---21----------
	----1--1-1---- - -
SCONCE Henry	------1--------
	11---1--------- - -
SCOTT Absalom	1---1--------
	---11--1------ - -
SCOTT Andrew	11---1--------
	12--1--------- - -
SCOTT Elijah	2121--1-------
	1------1------ - -
SCOTT James M	11--1---------
	-1--1--------- - -
SCOTT John	-------------
	-------------- - 6
SCOTT John C	2111-1--------
	--1-2--------- - -
SCOTT Thomas	1--1----1-----
	--121--1------ - -
SCOTT Thomas Jr	21---1--------
	------1------- - -
SCOTT Timothy	1--11---------
	----2--------- - -
SCOTT William	-3-1-1--------
	11111-1------- - -
SEARS Barton	----1----------
	----1--------- - -
SEARS Elizabeth	-----22--------
	---2----1----- - -
SEARS Jonas	113--1--------
	11---1--------- - -
SEARS Michael	1-11--1-------
	-1-1-1--------- - -
SECREST William *	----3-1-------
	-1--1--------- 1 -
SELBY Henry	--1----1------
	--2111-------- - -
SELLERS John	1--11---------
	1---1--------- - -
SERGEANT James	211--1--------
	----1--------- - -
SHANKLAND Andrew	111--1--------
	112--1--------- - -
SHANKLAND Benjamin	-11----1------
	--11---1------ - -
SHANKLAND James R	2-1-11--------
	-11-1---1--- - -
SHANKLAND John Jr	-22--1--------
	1-111--------- - -
SHANNON Jane *	-11-----------
	-----1-------- 2 -
SHANNON Robert	111--1--------
	11--1--------- 1 -
SHANNON Samuel	-11---1-------
	11-1--1------- - -
SHANNON Thomas	1---1---------
	----1--------- - -
SHARP John W	1----1--------
	-2--1--------- 3 -
SHARP William *	----1---------
	---1---------- - -
SHAW Ann	--------------
	2-1-1--------- - -
SHAW James	----1---------
	-----1-------- - -
SHAW Lewis	1111-1--------
	1-1111-------- - -
SHELY David	2---1---------
	----1--------- - -
SHELY David	---22--1------
	---1--1------- - -
SHEPARD Elizabeth	-------------
	----------1--- - -
SHIELDS Baker	211--1--------
	11--1--------- - -
SHULSE Abraham	--1---1-------
	1-3-1--------- - -
SHULSE Henry	-111--1-------
	2--1--1------- - -
SHUMATE Peyton	-------1------
	-------1------ 4 -
SIMS Rachel	---1----------
	-2-1--1------- 3 -
SIMS Thomas	-1211-1-------
	-1-1--1------- 1 -
SIX David	---2--1-------
	---1--1------- - -
SLED Nelson	2---1---------
	---1---1------ - -
SLOOP Margaret	--------------
	----------1--- - -
SLOOP Moses	--1-1---------
	11--1--------- - -
SMALL Joseph	----2---------
	1---1--------- - -
SMALL William	-----1--------
	-------------- - -
SMART Elijah	111---1-------
	-13---1------- - -
SMART Humphrey	--113--1------
	--11---1------ - -

SMART Humphrey Jr	1---1---------
	1--1--------- - -
SMART Matilda	11-----------
	11---1------- 2 -
SMART Sally	11-1-1-------
	--2---1------- - -
SMEDLEY Andrew J	----1-------
	1--1--------- - -
SMEDLEY Aron *	2-----1------
	------------- 2 -
SMITH Daniel	-----1-------
	-2--1--------- - -
SMITH David	1-1--1-------
	-----1------- - -
SMITH Elizabeth	-------------
	---------1---- 1 -
SMITH Henry	--------1-----
	--------1----- - -
SMITH Hiram	-1---1-------
	12---1--- - -
SMITH James	-1--------1---
	-----------1-- 5 -
SMITH Jetson	1-1--1-------
	--1--1--------- 3 -
SMITH Martha	1------------
	12--1--------- - -
SMITH Mitchell	----1---1----
	-----2--1------ - -
SMITH Paul	-----1-------
	---1--------- - -
SMITH Peter	1---1---------
	----1--------- - -
SMITH Samuel	1211-1-------
	--2--1--------- 7 -
SMITH Thomas	----2---------
	1--11--------- - -
SMITHERS John	--1--1---------
	-21---1------- - -
SMITHERS Sarah	-------------
	------------- 1 1
SNAP Daniel	--111--1-----
	--1--1--------- - -
SNAP Elijah	1121--1------
	11-1-1------- - -
SNAP Jacob	2-2---1-------
	-2--1--1---- - -
SNAP Peter	121--1-------
	1-1--1--------- - -
SNAP Peter	-----------1--
	-----------1-- - -
SNAP Samuel	1---1---------
	21--1--------- - -
SNAP Samuel	--------1-----
	----1-1------- 1 -
SNAP Willis	----1-------
	----1--------- - -
SNELLING Benjamin	11--1---------
	----1--------- - -
SOSBEE Robert	----11-------
	32--1--------- - -
SOSBEE Thomas	----------1---
	----------1--- - -
SOSBEE Thomas	1111---1------
	1-1--1--------- - -
SPARKS Catherine	-------------
	----2-1--1---- - -

SPARKS Charles	------1-------
	----1--------- - -
SPARKS George	------1-------
	2---2-1------- - 1
SPARKS Jonas	-12---1-------
	---1-1--------- - -
SPARKS Otho	21---1-------
	----1--------- - -
SPARKS William	---1---1------
	-221--1------- - -
SPENCER James	-1-----1-------
	32--1--------- 6 -
SPHAR Henry	----21--1-----
	----4--------- 1 -
SPICER Allen	-111-1-------
	-2-1-1--------- 1 -
SPICER Hiram	222-11-------
	11--1--------- 1 -
SPRATT Andrew	---21
	--12--1--------- - -
SPURGIN David M *	1---1---------
	----1--------- - -
SQUIRES James	1----1-------
	----1--------- 3 -
SQUIRES Mary	-12----------
	-11--1---------
SROUT Andrew	----1---------
	1---1--------- - -
ST THOMAS John F L *	------1-------
	----1--------- - -
STADLER William	--1-----1-----
	-------1----- - -
STANDIFORD James	--22---1------
	---1----1----- - -
STANDIFORD John	----1--1-----
	-----1--------- - -
STARK Rachel	-------------
	------------- - 1
STEPHENSON George	---1-----1----

STEPHENSON John	----1---------
	1---1---------
STEPHENSON Robert	--2-11-------
	12---1--------- - -
STEPHENSON Robert	---11--1------
	--2-1--------- - -
STEPHENSON Thomas M *	----2-1------
	12-1-1--------- 1 1
STEPHENSON William	----1---------

STERMAN Elizabeth	-------------
	----1---1----- 1 -
STEVESON Leonard	-------------
	------------- - 4
STEWART Abel	---------1----
	--------1----- - -
STEWART James	----2--1------
	--1-2-1------- 2 -
STEWART William *	--1--1-------
	111---------- 2 1
STITT James	1111--1------
	1111--1------- 2 1
STITT Mary	----1---------
	---------1---- 1 -
STITT Samuel	11---1---------
	1------1------- 1 -

```
STOKER Archibald          11---11--------
                          2---1--------- - -
STOKER Edward             --------1-----
                          --------1----- - -
STOKER Edward Jr          11--------1---
                          -----1-------- - -
STOKER James              -2---1--------
                          1-1-1-------- - -
STOKER Joseph             -------1------
                          ----1-1------- 1 -
STOKER William            1-1--1-1------
                          -21-----1----- - -
STOKES Hannah             -311----------
                          1-12-1-------- - -
STOKES Michah             --------------
                          ----1-1------- - -
STOKES Thomas S           ------1-------
                          ------1------- - -
STONE Asa L               -1--1---------
                          -1--1--------- 4 -
STOOPS James D            -1-1--1-------
                          --22--1------- - -
STOOPS John Jr            ----1---------
                          ---11--1------ - -
STOOPS John S             1---1---------
                          ---1---------- - -
STOOPS William            -22---1-------
                          21112-1------- - -
STOOPS William            ----1---------
                          12--1--------- - -
STORY Samuel              1---1---------
                          11-11-------- - -
STOUT Benjamin            --------------
                          -------------- 5 1
SUDDUTH John              -1-13--1------
                          1221--1------- - -
SUITS Nathan              ----1---------
                          ----1--------- - -
SUMMETT Archibald *       ----2---1-----
                          ----3--------- 2 1
SUMMETT Elijah            -11---1-------
                          212--1------- 1 -
SUMMETT Jacob             --1----1------
                          --11---------- - -
SUMMETT Jacob             --1----1------
                          --11---------- - -
SUMMETT James             1-11--1-------
                          -2-12-1------- - -
SWART George              1-11--1-------
                          1122---------- 2 -
SWART Jacob               3----1--------
                          -1---1-------- - -
SWART Margaret            ----1---------
                          -----1--1----- - -
TALBERT Mason             ---11---------
                          1---1--------- 2 -
TANNER Elizabeth          --121---------
                          --112-1------- - -
TANNER Johnathan          1---1---------
                          1--1--------- 1 -
TATEMAN Vincent           12-1--1-------
                          1-12--1------- - -
TAYLOR Benjamin           1--11---------
                          22--1--------- - -
TAYLOR George             -----1--1-----
                          ---11--1------ - -

TAYLOR George             2---1---------
                          ----1--------- - -
TAYLOR Hillery            22-2--1-------
                          --211-1-----1- - -
TAYLOR Jerome             ----2---------
                          ---1---------- - -
TAYLOR John               -111---1------
                          --111--------- - -
TAYLOR Thomas             11-1----------
                          ----1--------- - -
TEAL Asberry *            ----1---------
                          ----1--------- - -
TEAL Benjamin *           1--1-1--------
                          1---1--------- - -
TERRY Reuben              ----------1---
                          ----------1--- 8 -
THOMAS James              113---1-------
                          11---1-------- 3 -
THOMAS James              1-3---1-------
                          11---1-------- - -
THOMAS Lydia              ---11---------
                          ----11-1------ 1 -
THOMAS William            1----1--------
                          1----1-------- - -
THOMPSON Henry            --121--1------
                          -1----11------ 9 -
THROCKMORTEN Thomas       ---11---------
                          1---11--1----- 6 -
THROCKMORTON John         12---1--------
                          11--1-------- 2 -
THROCKMORTON John         ---1-----1----
                          --11--1------- 8 -
THROCKMORTON William M    -----1--------
                          -------------- 2 -
TILTON Jesse L            -2---1--------
                          1-1--1-------- - -
TILTON Richard            --1---1-------
                          -12---1------- - -
TIPET James A             -1--1---------
                          3---1--------- - -
TRIGG Ezekiel             ---1-1--------
                          --1--1-------- - -
TRIGG Samuel              ----1---------
                          2---1--------- - -
TRIMBLE David             121---1-------
                          111--1-------- - -
TRIMBLE Henry T           -----1--------
                          1----1-------- 2 -
TROUTMAN George           2--1--1-------
                          -12-111------- 1 -
TUNE Samuel               11----1-------
                          1---1-----1--- 4 -
TUREMAN Joseph F *        2111--1-------
                          --11-1-------- 3 -
TURLEY John               2--2--1-------
                          112--1-------- 5 -
TUTTLE Peter              --111--1------
                          -1-12--1------ - -
TWEEDY Letticia           --------------
                          --1-1---1----- 6 -
UTTERBACK Harman          -----------1--
                          ----1--1------ - -
VANKIRK Matthew           --22--1-------
                          112--1-------- - -
VARNER Noah               -1-11---------
                          2---1--------- - -
```

Name	Line 1	Line 2		Name	Line 1	Line 2
VAUGHAN Hannah	22111---------	--21--1-1---- - -		WAUGH SAmuel	2--1---------	1---1--------- - -
VAUGHAN John	2-1---1------	-2--1--------- - -		WAUGH Samuel M	----------1--	--------1---- 2 -
VAUGHAN Thomas	2--4--1------	-12--1-------- - -		WAUGH Thompson	-1--1---------	2---1--------- 2 -
VICTOR Ambrose	-1--11-------	21--1--------- 1 -		WEAVER Cornelius	--11---1-----	-1----1------ - -
VICTOR John	---1--1------	--11--1------- 5 -		WEAVER Reuben	----11-------	1---1--------- - -
VICTOR William	--21----1----	--------1---- 5 -		WEAVER Thomas	--1-1---1----	----1-1------ - -
VIMONT Franklin	-1-1-1-------	211--1-------- D -		WEAVER William	----1--------	1---1--------- - -
WAGGONER Daniel	1---1--------	----1-------- - -		WEAVER William	----1--------	1---1--------- - -
WAGGONER Godfrey	1---1--------	----1-------- - -		WEBB Charles	---21---1----	---11--------- 7 -
WAGGONER John	-221--1------	2----1-------- - -		WEBB Newton	----1--------	1--1---------- 1 -
WAKEFIELD Enoch	------1------	------------- - -		WELLS Andrew	----1--------	---1----------
WALCH Jacob	--------1----	--------1----		WELLS Daniel	----1--------	1---1--------- - -
WALLACE John	311---1------	---1-1-------- - -		WELLS Nathan	11--1--------	11----1------ - -
WALLACE Joseph B	21---1-------	-1---1-------- - -		WELLS Uriah	--21-1-------	1---1--------- - -
WALLACE William	------1------	------------- - -		WELLS William	1---1--------	-12--2-------- - -
WALLS James	2---1--------	---1---------- - -		WEST Adam	32--1--------	11--1-1------ - -
WALLS John	1---1--------	-1--1--------- - -		WEST Amos	1-221-1------	----1----1---
WALLS Reuben	-----------1--	---1--1-------		WEST Elijah *	---1-----1---	11---1-------- 4 -
WARD James	2---1--------	1--1---------- 1 -		WEST Philip	111-1--------	--11---1----- - -
WARD Solomon G	---3-----1---	--2----------- 2 -		WEST Robert	--1-2-1------	11--111------ - -
WARDLOW William	----1--------	22---1-------- - -		WHALEY Charles	22-1-11------	-1--11-------- - -
WARREN David	-1--1--------	1---1--------- - -		WHALEY Hiram	1-1-2--------	2--1-1-------- E -
WARREN Isaac	1---1--------	----1--------- - -		WHEATLY Josiah	11--1--------	3-3---2------ - -
WARREN Matthias	-1--1--1-----	1-223--1----- - -		WHEELER Aron	-1---1-------	1---1--------- 5 -
WASSON Barton	1---1--------	-1---1-------- - -		WHEELER Joseph	1---1--------	1---1--------- 1 -
WASSON Charles	21----1------	-1---1-------- 1 -		WHEELER Samuel D	11--1--------	1---1--------- - -
WASSON John	11--1-1------	12---1-------- - -		WHEELER Samuel D	1---1--1-----	1---1---------
WASSON Levi	-------2------	1------------- 4 -		WHITAKER James	1---1--------	--1----1--1-- - -
WATKINS Samuel	1121--1------	11--1--------- - -		WHITE Lewis	---1---1-----	1-1--1------- 2 -
WATTS George	-----1-------	22--1--------- - -		WHITE William	21--1--------	----1--------- - -
WATTS Ruth	----1--------	------------- - -		WIATT Charlott	3---1--------	-------------
WAUGH Archer S	2-11-1-------	1-21-1-------- 3 -		WIATT Elizabeth	--11-1---1---	-------------
WAUGH Luther	-1---1-------	-1--1--------- 1 -		WIGGINS Archibald	----------11-	-2--1-1------ 1 -
						2-22-1-------- - -

WIGGINS Cornelius	12-1--1-------	
	----1--1------	_ _
WIGGINS William	-121---1------	
	---11-1-------	2 -
WIGGINS William	------2--------	
	11-1-1--------	_ _
WILCOXEN William	3---1---------	
	----1---------	_ _
WILLIAMS Bird	11--1---------	
	1---1---------	_ _
WILLIAMS David B	-------1------	
	1313--1-------	3 -
WILLIAMS Ezkl	12---1--------	
	2---1---1----	_ _
WILLIAMS Green	--1--1--------	
	21---1-1------	_ _
WILLIAMS Samuel	-1---1--------	
	------1--------	_ _
WILLIAMS Samuel	1-221-1-------	
	12---1--------	D -
WILLIAMS Sanford	--23-1--------	
	---1--1-------	_ _
WILLIAMS Sarah	-11-1---------	
	11111-1-------	1 -
WILLS Archibald	1---1---------	
	----1---------	_ _
WILSON Charles	----1-----1---	
	1---1---------	_ _
WILSON David	--21--1-------	
	-111--1-------	_ _
WILSON Jesse	----1--1------	
	----1--1------	_ _
WILSON John	1----1--------	
	1---1---------	_ _
WILSON John	1----1--------	
	12--1---------	_ _
WILSON John	--2---1-------	
	2----1--------	_ 1
WILSON Melinda A	--1-----------	
	-1---1--------	_ _
WILSON Thomas	---11-11------	
	--21---1------	_ _
WILSON Thomas C	----1---------	
	1---1---------	_ _
WILSON William	------1-------	
	-------------	_ _
WILSON William	----1---------	
	----1---------	1 -
WILSON William	2-1-1---------	
	----1---------	_ _
WOLF James	---14---------	
	----1---------	_ _
WOOD Caleb	1---1---------	
	---1----------	_ _
WOOD George	----2---------	
	-1-----1------	_ _
WOOD John	-1--------1--	
	-111-1--------	4 -
WOOD John	-------------	
	-------------	_ 1
WOOD Nimrod	3-11--1-------	
	-21---1-------	8 -
WOOD Thomas J	----1---------	
	----1---------	_ _
WOOD William	--131--1------	
	-2-----1------	_ _
WOODARD Isaac	-------------	
	-------------	_ 3
WOODS Joseph	--11--1-------	
	--113--11-----	_ _
WORKMAN Michael	211--1--------	
	--111---------	_ _
WORNWAY Thomas	1---1---------	
	1---1---------	1 -
WRIGHT James	----21--------	
	-------------	7 -
YATES Milton	----1---------	
	11--1---------	_ _
YATES Samson	121--1--------	
	1---1---------	_ _
YAZEL Daniel	1---1---------	
	2----1--------	_ _
YOUNG Robert C	--3--1--------	
	--1--1--------	3 -